THE
KIOWA

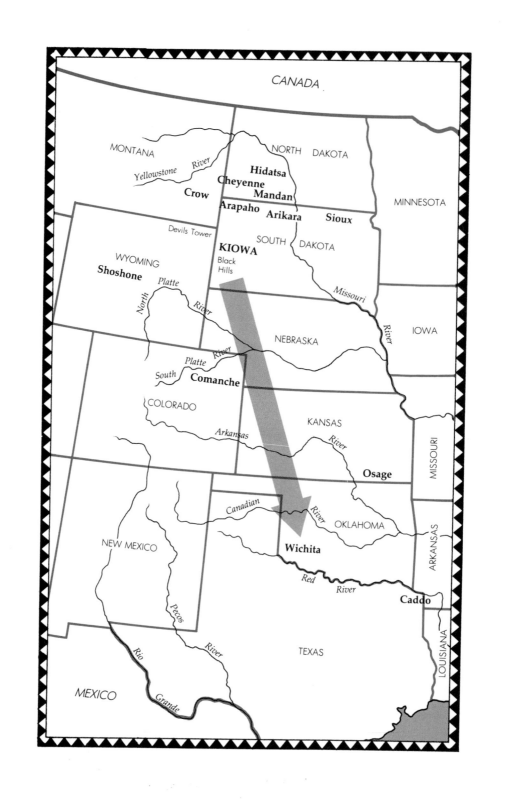

THE
KIOWA

John R. Wunder

Frank W. Porter III
General Editor

CHELSEA HOUSE PUBLISHERS
New York   Philadelphia

On the cover The buffalo-picture tipi that belonged to Kiowa tribe member Never Got Shot.

Chelsea House Publishers
Editor-in-Chief   Nancy Toff
Executive Editor   Remmel T. Nunn
Managing Editor   Karyn Gullen Browne
Copy Chief   Juliann Barbato
Picture Editor   Adrian G. Allen
Art Director   Maria Epes
Manufacturing Manager   Gerald Levine

Indians of North America
Senior Editor   Marjorie P. K. Weiser

Staff for **THE KIOWA**
Assistant Editor   Karen Schimmel
Deputy Copy Chief   Ellen Scordato
Copy Editor   Nicole Bowen
Editorial Assistant   Claire Wilson
Assistant Art Director   Laurie Jewell
Designer   Donna Sinisgalli
Design Assistant   James Baker
Picture Researcher   Alan Gottlieb
Production Coordinator   Joseph Romano

5   7   9   8   6   4

Library of Congress Cataloging-in-Publication Data

Wunder, John R.
The Kiowa.
(Indians of North America)
Bibliography: p.
Includes index.
Summary: Examines the history, culture, and changing fortunes of the Kiowa Indians.
1. Kiowa Indians. [1. Kiowa Indians. 2. Indians of North America] I. Title. II. Series: Indians of North America (Chelsea House Publishers)
E99.K5W85   1989   973'.0497   88-30159
ISBN   1-55546-710-5
       0-7910-0383-3 (pbk.)

CONTENTS

INDIANS OF NORTH AMERICA

The Abenaki

The Apache

The Arapaho

The Archaeology
  of North America

The Aztecs

The Blackfoot

The Cahuilla

The Catawbas

The Cherokee

The Cheyenne

The Chickasaw

The Chinook

The Chipewyan

The Choctaw

The Chumash

The Coast Salish Peoples

The Comanche

The Creeks

The Crow

Federal Indian Policy

The Hidatsa

The Hopi

The Huron

The Innu

The Inuit

The Iroquois

The Kiowa

The Kwakiutl

The Lenapes

Literatures of the
  American Indian

The Lumbee

The Maya

The Menominee

The Modoc

The Mohawk

The Nanticoke

The Narragansett

The Navajos

The Nez Perce

The Ojibwa

The Osage

The Paiute

The Pawnee

The Pima-Maricopa

The Potawatomi

The Powhatan Tribes

The Pueblo

The Quapaws

The Sac and Fox

The Santee Sioux

The Seminole

The Shawnee

The Shoshone

The Tarahumara

The Teton Sioux

The Tunica-Biloxi

Urban Indians

The Wampanoag

Women in American
  Indian Society

The Yakima

The Yankton Sioux

The Yuma

The Zuni

CHELSEA HOUSE PUBLISHERS

INDIANS OF NORTH AMERICA: CONFLICT AND SURVIVAL

Frank W. Porter III

*The Indians survived our
open intention of wiping them
out, and since the tide turned
they have even weathered
our good intentions toward them,
which can be much more deadly.*

John Steinbeck
America and Americans

When Europeans first reached the North American continent, they found hundreds of tribes occupying a vast and rich country. The newcomers quickly recognized the wealth of natural resources. They were not, however, so quick or willing to recognize the spiritual, cultural, and intellectual riches of the people they called Indians.

The Indians of North America examines the problems that develop when people with different cultures come together. For American Indians, the consequences of their interaction with non-Indian people have been both productive and tragic. The Europeans believed they had "discovered" a "New World," but their religious bigotry, cultural bias, and materialistic world view kept them from appreciating and understanding the people who lived in it. All too often they attempted to change the way of life of the indigenous people. The Spanish conquistadores wanted the Indians as a source of labor. The Christian missionaries, many of whom were English, viewed them as potential converts. French traders and trappers used the Indians as a means to obtain pelts. As Francis Parkman, the 19th-century historian, stated, "Spanish civilization crushed the Indian; English civilization scorned and neglected him; French civilization embraced and cherished him."

Nearly 500 years later, many people think of American Indians as curious vestiges of a distant past, waging a futile war to survive in a Space Age society. Even today, our understanding of the history and culture of American Indians is too often derived from unsympathetic, culturally biased, and inaccurate reports. The American Indian, described and portrayed in thousands of movies, television programs, books, articles, and government studies, has either been raised to the status of the "noble savage" or disparaged as the "wild Indian" who resisted the westward expansion of the American frontier.

7

Where in this popular view are the real Indians, the human beings and communities whose ancestors can be traced back to ice-age hunters? Where are the creative and indomitable people whose sophisticated technologies used the natural resources to ensure their survival, whose military skill might even have prevented European settlement of North America if not for devastating epidemics and the disruption of the ecology? Where are the men and women who are today diligently struggling to assert their legal rights and express once again the value of their heritage?

The various Indian tribes of North America, like people everywhere, have a history that includes population expansion, adaptation to a range of regional environments, trade across wide networks, internal strife, and warfare. This was the reality. Europeans justified their conquests, however, by creating a mythical image of the New World and its native people. In this myth, the New World was a virgin land, waiting for the Europeans. The arrival of Christopher Columbus ended a timeless primitiveness for the original inhabitants.

Also part of this myth was the debate over the origins of the American Indians. Fantastic and diverse answers were proposed by the early explorers, missionaries, and settlers. Some thought that the Indians were descended from the Ten Lost Tribes of Israel, others that they were descended from inhabitants of the lost continent of Atlantis. One writer suggested that the Indians had reached North America in another Noah's ark.

A later myth, perpetrated by many historians, focused on the relentless persecution during the past five centuries until only a scattering of these "primitive" people remained to be herded onto reservations. This view fails to chronicle the overt and covert ways in which the Indians successfully coped with the intruders.

All of these myths presented one-sided interpretations that ignored the complexity of European and American events and policies. All left serious questions unanswered. What were the origins of the American Indians? Where did they come from? How and when did they get to the New World? What was their life—their culture—really like?

In the late 1800s, anthropologists and archaeologists in the Smithsonian Institution's newly created Bureau of American Ethnology in Washington, D. C., began to study scientifically the history and culture of the Indians of North America. They were motivated by an honest belief that the Indians were on the verge of extinction and that along with them would vanish their languages, religious beliefs, technology, myths, and legends. These men and women went out to visit, study, and record data from as many Indian communities as possible before this information was forever lost.

By this time there was a new myth in the national consciousness. American Indians existed as figures in the American past. They had performed a historical mission. They had challenged white settlers who trekked across the continent. Once conquered, however, they were supposed to accept graciously the way of life of their conquerors.

The reality again was different. American Indians resisted both actively and passively. They refused to lose their unique identity, to be assimilated into white society. Many whites viewed the Indians not only as members of a conquered nation but also as "inferior" and "unequal." The rights of the Indians could be expanded, contracted, or modified as the conquerors saw fit. In every generation, white society asked itself what to do with the American Indians. Their answers have resulted in the twists and turns of federal Indian policy.

There were two general approaches. One way was to raise the Indians to a "higher level" by "civilizing" them. Zealous missionaries considered it their Christian duty to elevate the Indian through conversion and scanty education. The other approach was to ignore the Indians until they disappeared under pressure from the ever-expanding white society. The myth of the "vanishing Indian" gave stronger support to the latter option, helping to justify the taking of the Indians' land.

Prior to the end of the 18th century, there was no national policy on Indians simply because the American nation had not yet come into existence. American Indians similarly did not possess a political or social unity with which to confront the various Europeans. They were not homogeneous. Rather, they were loosely formed bands and tribes, speaking nearly 300 languages and thousands of dialects. The collective identity felt by Indians today is a result of their common experiences of defeat and/or mistreatment at the hands of whites.

During the colonial period, the British crown did not have a coordinated policy toward the Indians of North America. Specific tribes (most notably the Iroquois and the Cherokee) became military and political pawns used by both the crown and the individual colonies. The success of the American Revolution brought no immediate change. When the United States acquired new territory from France and Mexico in the early 19th century, the federal government wanted to open this land to settlement by homesteaders. But the Indian tribes that lived on this land had signed treaties with European governments assuring their title to the land. Now the United States assumed legal responsibility for honoring these treaties.

At first, President Thomas Jefferson believed that the Louisiana Purchase contained sufficient land for both the Indians and the white population.

9

Within a generation, though, it became clear that the Indians would not be allowed to remain. In the 1830s the federal government began to coerce the eastern tribes to sign treaties agreeing to relinquish their ancestral land and move west of the Mississippi River. Whenever these negotiations failed, President Andrew Jackson used the military to remove the Indians. The southeastern tribes, promised food and transportation during their removal to the West, were instead forced to walk the "Trail of Tears." More than 4,000 men, women, and children died during this forced march. The "removal policy" was successful in opening the land to homesteaders, but it created enormous hardships for the Indians.

By 1871 most of the tribes in the United States had signed treaties ceding most or all of their ancestral land in exchange for reservations and welfare. The treaty terms were intended to bind both parties for all time. But in the General Allotment Act of 1887, the federal government changed its policy again. Now the goal was to make tribal members into individual landowners and farmers, encouraging their absorption into white society. This policy was advantageous to whites who were eager to acquire Indian land, but it proved disastrous for the Indians. One hundred thirty-eight million acres of reservation land were subdivided into tracts of 160, 80, or as little as 40 acres, and allotted to tribe members on an individual basis. Land owned in this way was said to have "trust status" and could not be sold. But the surplus land—all Indian land not allotted to individuals— was opened (for sale) to white settlers. Ultimately, more than 90 million acres of land were taken from the Indians by legal and illegal means.

The resulting loss of land was a catastrophe for the Indians. It was necessary to make it illegal for Indians to sell their land to non-Indians. The Indian Reorganization Act of 1934 officially ended the allotment period. Tribes that voted to accept the provisions of this act were reorganized, and an effort was made to purchase land within preexisting reservations to restore an adequate land base.

Ten years later, in 1944, federal Indian policy again shifted. Now the federal government wanted to get out of the "Indian business." In 1953 an act of Congress named specific tribes whose trust status was to be ended "at the earliest possible time." This new law enabled the United States to end unilaterally, whether the Indians wished it or not, the special status that protected the land in Indian tribal reservations. In the 1950s federal Indian policy was to transfer federal responsibility and jurisdiction to state governments, encourage the physical relocation of Indian peoples from reservations to urban areas, and hasten the termination, or extinction, of tribes.

Between 1954 and 1962 Congress passed specific laws authorizing the termination of more than 100 tribal groups. The stated purpose of the termination policy was to ensure the full and complete integration of Indians into American society. However, there is a less benign way to interpret this legislation. Even as termination was being discussed in Congress, 133 separate bills were introduced to permit the transfer of trust land ownership from Indians to non-Indians.

With the Johnson administration in the 1960s the federal government began to reject termination. In the 1970s yet another Indian policy emerged. Known as "self-determination," it favored keeping the protective role of the federal government while increasing tribal participation in, and control of, important areas of local government. In 1983 President Reagan, in a policy statement on Indian affairs, restated the unique "government to government" relationship of the United States with the Indians. However, federal programs since then have moved toward transferring Indian affairs to individual states, which have long desired to gain control of Indian land and resources.

As long as American Indians retain power, land, and resources that are coveted by the states and the federal government, there will continue to be a "clash of cultures," and the issues will be contested in the courts, Congress, the White House, and even in the international human rights community. To give all Americans a greater comprehension of the issues and conflicts involving American Indians today is a major goal of this series. These issues are not easily understood, nor can these conflicts be readily resolved. The study of North American Indian history and culture is a necessary and important step toward that comprehension. All Americans must learn the history of the relations between the Indians and the federal government, recognize the unique legal status of the Indians, and understand the heritage and cultures of the Indians of North America.

Buffalo Chase, *a notebook drawing by Wo-haw, one of several
Kiowa warriors imprisoned at Fort Marion, Florida, around 1875.
The buffalo, or American bison, provided food, clothing, fuel, shelter, and tools for the Plains Indians until it was hunted into near
extinction by the late 19th century.*

EMERGING— EARLIEST TIMES TO 1700

Behold! I am alive! I am alive!"

These are the words of N. Scott Momaday, a 20th-century Kiowa poet and chronicler. His exclamation might well have been spoken by the first Americans entering the New World tens of thousands of years ago. Twelve thousand or more years ago the Kiowa's ancestors migrated from Asia, walking across a land bridge that today is covered by the waters of the Bering Strait separating Alaska and Siberia. At that time, glaciers covered more than half of North America, Europe, and Asia. As the climate changed, alternately warming and cooling, these huge sheets of ice melted and refroze. As they did, they reshaped the land in their path, carving lakes and rivers, valleys and flatlands into the once-submerged terrain.

During this period, known as the Ice Age, much of what is now the central and eastern United States lay under a sheet of ice known as the Wisconsin Glacier, which reached as far south as what is now the state of Kansas. When this glacier began to melt about 18,000 years ago, spruce trees sprang up on much of the land that had previously been under ice. The climate continued to become warmer and drier, however, and eventually the spruce trees could not survive in the new environment. Gradually they were replaced by leaf-bearing trees such as the cottonwood. About 10,000 years ago the cottonwoods died out as well. In their place appeared the vast grasslands that today make up the American Great Plains.

Botanists and geologists, meteorologists and geographers alike, tell us that the Plains was once two different forests before it became one of the world's largest grasslands. In important ways, the Kiowa's creation beliefs match the geological and historical interpretations of their origin. Their living history includes accounts of the creation of their immediate environment and origin of their people. Kiowa creation beliefs begin time with massive floods that were followed by severe fluctuations in climate. These changes resulted in the drying of the earth, the formation and subsequent destruction of forests, the spread of lush grassland, and the migration onto the North American Plains of the buffalo, or bison, and other animals. Intertwined with this evolution were the Kiowa.

The Kiowa originally called themselves *Kwu'da*, which means "pulling out." They also named themselves *Tep-da*, or "coming out." Scholars think that these early names reflected the Kiowa's beliefs about their origin. Much later their Comanche neighbors on the southern Plains called them *Kaigwa*, a Comanche word meaning roughly "two halves differ." This term likely referred to their appearance: At one time, Kiowa warriors cut their hair on only one side of their head, leaving that on the other side long. From *Kaigwa* eventually was derived the name *Kiowa*, which came to mean "the principal people" to the Kiowa.

According to N. Scott Momaday, he heard from his grandmother Aho the Kiowa tradition that their tribal migration to the Great Plains began when "they emerged from a sunless world." A supernatural being, Saynday, called the Kiowa into the world by tapping a stick on a hollow cottonwood log. Each tap brought forth another person until a pregnant woman became stuck in the hollow trunk, preventing any more Kiowa from coming through to join the first tribal members. Saynday then instructed these folk of the forest—a

people literally begot of a tree—how to hunt the bison and the antelope on the Great Plains.

Much of what is known about the environmental changes that occurred on the Great Plains thousands of years ago is the result of palynology, or pollen analysis. Palynologists study the changes in the plants of a region over a period of time. Through the microscopic examination of pollen grains that have remained damp since being deposited, they can often determine the changes in climate that took place even thousands of years ago. Because the Great Plains is quite dry, only a few ancient pollen deposits have remained moist in some former lake beds. But enough sites on the Great Plains have been found to show that the spruce forests gave way in the south approximately 12,000 years ago and in the northern and eastern borderland areas about 9,500 years ago. The grasses first covered the north central Plains and spread north and east, away from the Rocky Mountains.

It was during the transition from forests to grasslands that the earliest ancestors of the Plains Indians first ventured onto the Great Plains. They remained on the edge of the Plains for thousands of years, only occasionally penetrating the region to hunt. These people, known to us as Paleo-Indians (*Paleo* means old or ancient), were nomadic hunters who followed deer, bison, and other game from one place to another. Over time, however, the Paleo-Indians developed a way of life that was tied to a specific area, collecting wild plants and nuts and hunting animals that appeared in their immediate environment.

Plains Indian culture evolved into two distinct types. Some groups, having adopted the techniques of farming from their neighbors to the south, became a settled people, raising corn, beans, and squash and supplementing this diet by hunting and gathering. Others remained primarily buffalo hunters, obtaining the bulk of their food supply when the massive herds migrated through their hunting territory each year. Among these were the Kiowa.

Although the Kiowa relied largely on the game they could obtain from their surroundings, often they traded surplus animal skins for corn and other foodstuffs raised by agricultural Indians. They maintained good trade relations with the Arikara, Hidatsa, and Mandan tribes, in particular, who lived in permanent villages along the Missouri River. Unlike these settled agriculturalists, the Kiowa and the other nomadic Plains hunters changed locations frequently to keep up with the shifting patterns of the animals they hunted. They lived in tipis, which were portable and consisted of a buffalo hide covering fastened to a frame made of wooden poles.

The tipi and other possessions were transported from place to place by means of the *travois*, an A-shaped support. The narrow end of the platform was attached to a harness on the back

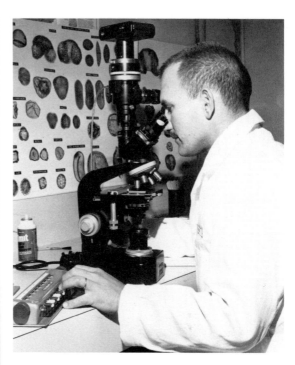

Dr. Vaughn M. Bryant, Jr., of Texas A&M University, is an archaeological palynologist, a scientist who analyzes prehistoric pollen. Pollen grains from archaeological sites can provide clues to plants used by people who lived thousands of years ago.

of an animal, and the wide end dragged along the ground as the animal pulled the travois and its load. The tipi poles themselves served as the main frame of the carrier, and the cover and other belongings were strapped across this frame. For many years dogs were used to pull the travois. Then in the early 17th century another animal appeared that proved much more efficient—the horse.

Although horses had thrived in North America, by the time the first Pa-

The nomadic Plains Indians used a travois to transport their possessions. The load was lashed to crossbars between two poles, whose back ends trailed on the ground. Travois were originally harnessed to dogs but were later adapted for horses.

leo-Indians arrived the animal had become extinct. It was only in the early 1500s, when Spanish conquistadores brought horses with them to aid in the exploration of Mexico, that the animal could be found in America again. Eventually the explorers ventured north into what is now New Mexico, and this is where the Indians of the southern Plains were introduced to the magnificent animal. Soon Indians on the northern Plains, including the Kiowa, were riding horses as well.

The horse's appearance among the Plains tribes was not just a matter of exchanging one beast of burden for a larger and better one: Its addition to Plains Indian culture had ramifications that touched every aspect of the Indians' way of life. It was only then that the stereotype of the Plains Indian emerged—the warrior acrobatically perched on a galloping horse, chasing down buffalo or enemy warriors. James Mooney, a 19th-century ethnologist for the Smithsonian Institution, described the Plains Indian before the advent of the horse:

> He was a half-starved skulker in the timber, creeping up on foot toward the unwary deer or building a brush corral with infinite labor to surround a herd of antelope, and seldom venturing more than a few days' journey from home. With the horse he was transformed into the daring

buffalo hunter, able to procure in a single day enough food to supply his family for a year, leaving him free then to sweep the plains with his war parties along a range of a thousand miles.

The horse revolutionized nomadic Plains life. It not only meant that Indians could secure more meat in less time and travel greater distances in search of food; it changed the entire focus of the Indians' way of life. The horse became a symbol of social status. Stealing horses from an enemy camp garnered one of the highest war honors a warrior could achieve. The family of a bride-to-be looked forward to receiving horses from her intended husband. The introduction of this new means of transportation made it possible for the various bands, or divisions, of a tribe to get together more frequently for tribal ceremonies and socializing. Distance was no longer a hindrance to communication. Even the size of tipis increased because horses could drag longer poles and heavier hide covers over varying terrain for countless miles.

It was as the embodiment of this horse-based way of life that the Kiowa culture flourished. In the earliest European reports describing the Kiowa with horses, they were said to be living in the Black Hills of western South Dakota during the 1700s.

The Kiowa's own tribal history tells of their origin near the headwaters of the Yellowstone and Missouri rivers, in what is now western Montana. It was there that the Kiowa emerged from the hollow cottonwood tree trunk and learned from Saynday the Plains Indian culture, according to Kiowa beliefs. After emerging from the hollow log, the Kiowa account continues, some of their ancestors intermarried with the Sarci Indians, who lived near the North Saskatchewan River in present-day Canada and spoke a language similar to that of the Apache Indians. These unions gave rise to the Kiowa-Apache, a separate but similar tribe that lived and traveled with the Kiowa but spoke a very different language.

At some point in the 17th century, a dispute between two opposing Kiowa leaders led to a split in the tribe. A female antelope had been slain in the hunt, and both chiefs laid claim to the animal's udder. The defeated leader took his band of followers and moved northwest. The subsequent fate of these people, thereafter called the *Azatanhop*, or angry travelers, is unknown. The rest of the Kiowa and Kiowa-Apache traveled southeast, crossing the Yellowstone River and taking up residence in the Black Hills of South Dakota, near land occupied by the Crow, Cheyenne, and Arapaho peoples.

This journey resulted in two significant happenings. First, the Kiowa obtained the horse, probably from the Crow after the Kiowa moved into the Black Hills region. Kiowa stories tell how they made the first horse, but it was thrown away to become *mankiah*, the whirlwind. Because the Kiowa made the whirlwind they have no fears of tornadoes and other storms on the Plains. They succeeded in a second attempt, fashioning a horse from a prairie dog's hide, a deer's ears, a turtle's hooves, an elk's teeth, and using a turkey's beard for a tail and a whirlwind's hair for the flank. In 1682 René-Robert Cavelier, Sieur de La Salle, the French explorer who was the first European to write of the Kiowa, saw them and the Kiowa-Apache with many horses, which they had obtained from the Spanish in Mexico. The Kiowa even-

Paintings on this buffalo hide portray many figures prominent in Kiowa legends. Most notable is (top center) Saynday, the supernatural being in human form who created the world. To his left are Thunder, depicted as a bird that causes lightning and thunder with its beak and wings, and Whirlwind, a winged horse with a body of clouds and the tail of a fish. Below them are two Zemoguani, great horned fish that, the Kiowa believed, lived in underwater caves and sometimes seized unlucky swimmers.

tually became known as expert horse riders of the Plains.

The second event of benefit to the Kiowa was a diplomatic alliance they made with the Crow, probably around 1700. This alliance protected the smaller Kiowa Nation and allowed it to prosper. It heralded the diplomatic successes the Kiowa would have in the future as noted orators and negotiators of the Great Plains.

Scientific study cannot confirm the tribe's claim that it originated on the northern Plains. As a result, there have been several theories of the tribe's origin and subsequent migration to the Black Hills. The ethnologist James Mooney, who lived among the tribe during the late 19th century, largely accepted the beliefs of the Kiowa about their early history.

More recent theories, however, have been based on comparison and analysis of the languages spoken by the Kiowa and other peoples in the Southwest and on the Plains. The Kiowa language is similar to the Tanoan languages spoken by the Taos and Jemez Pueblo Indians of New Mexico. For this reason, some linguists and anthropologists believe that the Kiowa originated on the southern and not the northern Plains and became a distinct people along the Rio Grande in what is now New Mexico. There a group of buffalo-hunting Kiowa met up with Tanoan-speaking people who lived in settled villages and depended on farming instead of hunting for much of their food. Some of these Tanoan-speakers abandoned their traditional farming and joined the Kiowa as nomadic buffalo hunters. Eventually the Kiowa-Tanoans and the Kiowa-Apache (who, according to this theory, are an offshoot of the Lipan Apache of present-day Texas) left their homeland on the southern Plains and moved north beyond the Black Hills. They then divided after the quarrel over the antelope's udder, with part of the tribe moving south to the Black Hills and some moving northwest. Although Kiowa accounts of having traded with the Taos and Jemez Pueblo Indians give some support to this version of their origin, this theory is generally not accepted by scholars of the Kiowa or by the Kiowa themselves.

A third theory of Kiowa origin, which combines the first two, takes into consideration both cultural and environmental factors such as language, Kiowa oral history, and cultural practices based on the resources of the Great Plains. It is perhaps the most plausible. Supporters of this theory contend that the ancestors of the Kiowa as well as of the Taos and Jemez Pueblo Indians had originally belonged to a single tribe that occupied the northern Plains. At some point in the very remote past this tribe divided. One part moved west of the Rocky Mountains into the Great Basin around Utah and Nevada, where they ultimately became speakers of a language belonging to a linguistic family known as Uto-Aztecan. The other part stayed on the northern Plains and came to speak a language of the Kiowa-Tanoan family. Around the year 1000 this

James Mooney (1861–1921) spent years among the Kiowa to learn about their way of life. Mooney was employed by the Bureau of American Ethnology in the late 19th century to record details of Indian cultures, which were recognized as undergoing irreversible changes.

group itself separated into the Tanoan and the Kiowan linguistic groups, with the Tanoan-speakers migrating south to New Mexico. Eventually the Kiowan-speakers moved southeast to the Black Hills, possibly as a result of the quarrel over the antelope.

However the Kiowa came to be on the northern Plains, by about 1700 they were firmly entrenched in the region around the Black Hills of South Dakota. They shared the dynamic way of life of the neighboring Plains peoples, a way of life that would serve them well for the next century and a half. ▲

Woman on a Horse, *a 1966 watercolor by Kiowa artist George Silverhorn.*

LIFE
ON THE
GREAT PLAINS

To be Kiowa in 1700 was to be a practicing member of the Plains Indian culture. Food, shelter, transportation, dress, art, religion, and social organization—all of these aspects of a way of life were practiced similarly by Native Americans inhabiting the Great Plains. For the Kiowa as for other Plains Indians, this culture was strongly influenced by their environment.

The Great Plains as a geographic region extends from Saskatchewan in the north to Texas in the south. During their history the Kiowa traversed the entire length of this region, which is characterized by lack of rainfall, lack of trees, and (except for the Black Hills) lack of distinctive topographical features. This flat, semiarid grassland experiences climatic extremes—temperatures may rise to 100 degrees Fahrenheit for 30 days straight or fall below 32 degrees Fahrenheit for just as long. It is not unusual for tornadoes and blizzards to blow up unexpectedly. The Plains is a harsh yet beautiful land that requires resilience and adaptability for survival.

Most of the Plains is covered by grasslands. Three types of grasses grow there, depending on the amount of precipitation: Tall grasses are found where annual rainfall is about 20 inches per year, short grasses require 10 to 20 inches, and desert shrub (also known as sagebrush) needs 10 inches per year. Tall and short grasses have long root systems that allow them to grow continuously, forming lush carpets.

No carpet of grass covers the Black Hills on the northern Plains, however. Here a timber island set in uneven topography provides a sanctuary for animals and humans alike. Most Plains Indian nations were attracted to the Black Hills because of its resources and its solitary uniqueness. The Black Hills, a shrine of forest, and the surrounding grasslands had become the home of the Kiowa by 1700.

The animals living on the Great Plains adjusted to the new environment. One animal dominated the Plains, and it came to dominate Kiowa life as well. This animal, the buffalo, served as a kind of commissary, or source of food and equipment, for the Plains Indians. No other animal was as crucial to their way of life, nor was any other animal as revered. The Indians' food, clothing, shelter, tools, fuel, weapons, and medicines all came from the buffalo. Their very survival depended upon it. Because the Plains Indians were so dependent on the buffalo, it became the focus of numerous social and religious practices.

Although the buffalo was the primary animal that the Kiowa hunted, other Plains animals, such as the antelope, jackrabbit, prairie dog, wolf, and coyote were also important. These animals had certain common characteristics that made them well adapted to life in this environment: Most were grass eaters and needed little water. All were fleet of foot. To kill animals with such traits called for special hunting techniques, which came to depend on the use of the bow and arrow and the horse.

The center of Kiowa life was hunting. Their very survival depended on it. Hunters went out in search of game both individually and in groups. One commonly used technique was that of

Indian hunters wearing wolf-skin disguises approach a buffalo herd in this painting by George Catlin.

disguising themselves by placing wolf skins over their backs. Then they would quietly sneak up on a buffalo and shoot it with arrows or spear it with lances. Collective hunts involved all of the men of a band or village. Sometimes the hunters ran shouting toward a herd of buffalo, crowding the frightened animals as they approached the edge of a cliff. Many buffalo fell over the edge and were either killed in the fall or sufficiently injured to be easily finished off with an arrow or spear. At other times the hunters set a circle of fire in the grass around a grazing herd. The animals usually panicked when they saw the flames and either trampled each other to death or were suffocated by the smoke.

After horses became available on the Plains, collective hunting techniques were adapted. Now a group of mounted hunters could separate a single buffalo from the herd and surround it. They could then shoot the animal with bows and arrows or lance it with spears. Because hunters on horseback were not in as great danger of being crushed beneath a stampeding buffalo herd as hunters on foot were, this method was safer than most others.

Collective hunts were carefully regulated by a select group of warriors, who were known as "Dog Soldiers" because a dog had appeared to each of them in a vision or dream. In addition to serving as guards on the hunt, the Dog Soldiers presided over tribal ceremonies and acted as camp police. Thomas Battey, the first non-Indian to teach and live among the Kiowa, described the role of these soldiers in his journal in 1873:

> Being determined that none of their thoughtless young men should go raiding in Texas, and thereby bring trouble upon the tribe, the Kiowas . . . organized a military system, under the control of the war chiefs, which was put immediately into operation. By this a strong guard of soldiers were continually watching, day and night, while in camp, to prevent any such enterprise from being undertaken. In moving from place to place, these soldiers marched on each side of the main body, while a front guard went before, and a rear guard behind, thus preventing any from straggling.

Their buffalo hunts were conducted in the same military order. The soldiers, going out first, surrounded a tract of country in which there was a large herd of buffalo; and no one might chase a buffalo past this perimeter on pain of having his horse shot by the soldiers.

The Dog Soldiers were chosen from among the military societies to which Kiowa warriors belonged. Young boys joined the *Polanyup*, or Rabbits. As they grew older and proved themselves as hunters and leaders and acquired war honors, they could progress through five warrior societies. War honors were earned for any one of 12 deeds, ranging from stealing the enemy's horses to charging the enemy's leading warrior. The highest honor of all was to touch, but not kill, an enemy warrior. A man

This young warrior is a member of the Rabbits, the first of five Kiowa warrior societies.

had to perform four such deeds in order to achieve the rank of warrior.

Only the 10 best warriors were admitted to the *Koitsenko*, the highest and most prestigious soldier society. Koitsenko members, like those of other societies, had to follow certain rules. Each warrior belonging to this exclusive group wore a long red sash and carried a sacred spear into battle. Once engaged with the enemy, he had to fix one end of his sash in the ground with his spear and fight from that position until another member released him. If it appeared that a Koitsenko warrior might be killed, the other members could tell him to advance, which actually meant he could retreat: According to the rules of the society, a person had to do the opposite of whatever was said. Or one member could release another by pulling the warrior's spear out of the ground, thus allowing him to retreat.

In addition to having ranked military societies, Kiowa society as a whole was organized by ranked social classes. People of the highest status formed the *onde*, which consisted of great warriors, major tribal leaders, and keepers of the tribe's religious objects. Wealth was an important credential, but it did not guarantee inclusion. Warriors and chiefs tended to gain wealth, especially horses, as they accomplished heroic deeds. Both men and women could become onde, to which about 10 percent of the tribe belonged. Next in rank was the *ondegup'a*, which comprised lesser warriors, minor tribal leaders, and people of limited wealth—about 40 percent of the tribe. Most Kiowa belonged to the *kaan*, or poor people. Only the *dapone*, those who lacked wealth and military experience, ranked lower.

The makeup of the classes was constantly changing. As men acquired war honors and earned recognition, they ascended the social ladder. However, they could descend just as easily. A person who lied, stole, or was cruel to another member of the tribe risked losing rank. A person who killed a fellow Kiowa was almost certain to be socially ostracized. Punishment was not always meted out equally; a person of the onde often did not lose rank for committing the same type of misdemeanor that caused a person of a lower class to be demoted. For the most part, men made the climb up the ladder to the onde. Women usually became part of this elite aristocracy only if they were born or married into it. They could, however, also be admitted because of exceptional skill in a craft, pleasing looks, or some noteworthy achievement.

Among the members of the onde were the tribe's leading chiefs. Each band, or subdivision, of the Kiowa was headed by a chief who made decisions concerning his band. Often one of these men would be a particularly respected leader as a result of his military and diplomatic abilities. Such a principal chief would come to have influence over all the Kiowa bands. From time to time these leaders met in council to discuss matters concerning the entire tribe, such as when and where to hold tribal ceremonies, whether to go to war, and when to make peace.

Most band chiefs were outstanding warriors, but some were equally noted spiritual leaders or medicine men. The Kiowa had various religious leaders to whom the people turned for guidance and cures. These leaders belonged to different religious societies, depending on the type of power they possessed. People who had the power to treat wounds belonged to the Buffalo Doctor Society; those who had the gift of prophecy were members of the Owl Doctor Society; those who guarded the tribe's most sacred object and the person who looked after it belonged to the Sun Dance Shield Society; and those who possessed the power of magic were members of the Eagle Shield Society. Only men could become members of these organizations. A select group of older women belonged to the Bear Women Society, a highly secretive organization.

The Kiowa seldom took any action without consulting a religious leader first. A war party heading out on a raid, for example, often included a member of the Owl Doctor Society to predict the outcome of the attack and a member of the Buffalo Doctor Society to attend to the warriors' wounds. Their methods of predicting and healing often combined physical elements, such as sweating and smoking, with spiritual ones, such as songs, dance, and ritual.

Each member of a religious society had his own rawhide medicine shield on which he had painted the symbol of the organization. The symbol for the Eagle Shield Society, for example, was a blue eagle and two blue guns on a yellow shield. Warriors also owned shields that they decorated with symbols of their personal medicine. Generally such shields were part of their war medicine and were not used to ward off blows by enemy warriors.

Twice a year the Kiowa recorded the most significant event to have occurred

(continued on page 28)

THE KIOWA'S PICTURE-
HISTORY OF THEIR TRIBE

Beginning in 1833, members of the Kiowa tribe kept a pictorial record of important events in their tribal history. Every year two key episodes were recorded, one from the winter and one from the summer. These winter and summer counts, as they were called, were originally painted on buffalo hide; as the buffalo became scarce, they were redrawn with colored pencils on heavy manila paper. The Kiowa, who lacked a means of writing their language, read each image as a reminder of the major events that had taken place during their history.

Below each image was a simple drawing to indicate whether the image referred to a winter or summer event. The winter images were marked by a black bar, symbolizing a dead blade of grass. The summer images were marked by a sketch of the sacred lodge, where the Sun Dance was held early every summer.

We know of the existence of four of these calendars. The first was kept by Settan ("Little Chief"), who in 1892 gave it to ethnologist James Mooney for safekeeping, saying that he "was now old and the young men were forgetting their history." This calendar spans 60 years, starting in 1833. Settan also revealed to Mooney the existence of another calendar kept by a tribe member named Anko. This included both a yearly record for 29 years beginning in 1864 and a monthly record for the last 37 months of that period. Anko's counts, which were drawn on the same buffalo hide, are usually considered to be two distinct calendars.

Mooney learned of the fourth calendar through Lieutenant Hugh Scott of the 7th U.S. Cavalry at Fort Sill, Oklahoma. This record was kept by Dohasan ("Little Bluff"), head chief of the Kiowa for more than 30 years. It had actually been started by Dohasan's uncle (of the same name) and was continued, following his death in 1866, by the nephew. It is believed that other calendars were kept, but they may have been buried with their creators.

These calendars did not always record those events of greatest importance to the whole tribe; sometimes the image drawn reflects only the personal remembrances of the chronicler. But even drawings of an apparently trivial incident served as memory aids in recalling greater events. During the winter evenings, the keeper of the calendar would issue an invitation to the other men to "come and smoke." While they passed the pipe, each man would recount the episodes evoked by the calendar's images, thus keeping the tribal past vivid in their memories.

Mooney found that where the calendars overlapped they were notably consistent in their accounts, which was a clear demonstration of their reliability. He used them in writing his own *Calendar History of the Kiowa Indians*, perhaps the first ethnography to rely on an Indian source of history in addition to ethnologists' usual reliance on oral interviews with Indians. The calendars, he wrote, show the "universal human instinct" to "preserve to future ages the memory of past achievements."

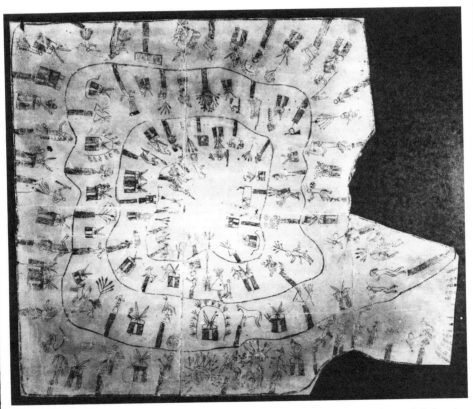

A Kiowa calendar drawn on heavy paper. The calendar begins at the lower left-hand corner (1833) and spirals inward, terminating at the center (1892).

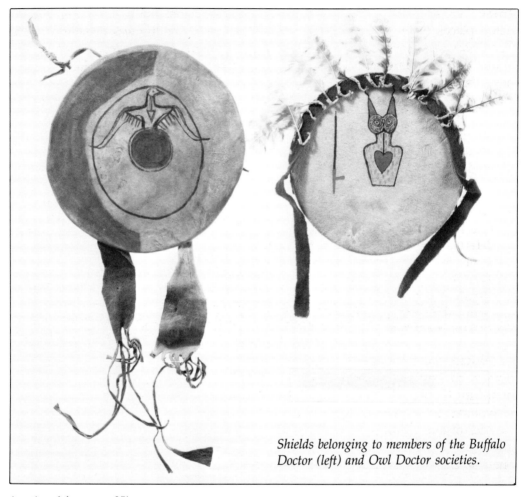

Shields belonging to members of the Buffalo Doctor (left) and Owl Doctor societies.

(continued from page 25)

during the previous six months. The Summer Count and the Winter Count constituted a kind of illustrated calendar or journal of Kiowa history. Every summer and every winter, the calendar's creator, usually one of the prominent leaders, drew images on a buffalo hide. The oldest calendar that the Kiowa can remember was buried with its creator around 1790. The oldest surviving calendar begins with the year 1833 and is the earliest written record of their past. For 60 years, from 1833 to 1893, this calendar chronicled the most turbulent era the Kiowa would know.

Kiowa men usually decorated their tipis as well. Some tipis were painted to match the warrior's shield, whereas others depicted celebrated exploits in war or on the hunt. Prominent families frequently had a design that, through the years, came to identify that family.

These "family tipis" occupied designated places in the camp circle of the Sun Dance, the Kiowa's most important annual event. According to James Mooney, their designs for the most part were

> [o]f so ancient an origin that the present members of the tribe cannot remember how they originated. In general they grew out of what the original designer claimed were visions. On dying, the warrior who held what was called the "tipi right" delegated it to some member of his family. When it happened that for any reason he failed in this, the design, or coat of arms, as it may be called, became extinct, as no one was allowed to revive it.

Although the honor of painting the tipis fell to the men of the tribe, the task of making them fell to the women. After a woman had accumulated enough treated, or tanned, hides to make a tipi cover, she cut them, making sure that they fit together properly. Then she sewed the individual hides together with buffalo sinew. A large tipi could measure more than 20 feet in diameter and require as many as 30 buffalo skins.

Women were also responsible for putting up and taking down the tipis wherever the band traveled. For the framework of the tipi, the Kiowa used three main poles, which proved especially sturdy against strong winds. After the 3 poles were set in the ground and tied securely together at the top, the women leaned as many as 16 more

poles against the basic frame. The diameter of the tipi was usually equal to the length of the poles, which on the average measured 14 feet long.

Thomas Battey, who during the 1870s spent almost 18 months among the Kiowa, wrote of their dwellings:

> The lodge . . . was built in the form of a conical tent, made by stretching several tanned buffalo skins, strongly sewed together, over poles set in a circle, crossing at the top in the centre, and fastened by thongs. The

A 1971 reconstruction of the 19th-century Do-Giagya-Guat, *or* Tipi of Battle Pictures, *by Kiowa artist Dixon Palmer. Kiowa men painted their tipis with designs that matched their shields or were inherited through family tradition.*

Buckskin dress decorated with rows of elk teeth, modeled by Ah-kaun-ah of the Kiowa in an 1870 Indian beauty contest. Kiowa clothing was often adorned with shells, bones, or porcupine quills.

tent, being raised and spread, is fastened down by pegs at the bottom. The entrance is a small hole opening towards the east, and covered by a piece of thick skin so tanned as to be somewhat stiff, and ornamented with paint. This is fastened, by buckskin strings, on whichever side the wind may happen to be, so as to form a self-closing door. The opening is not over three or four feet high, and does not extend to the ground, barely admitting a large man.

Battey went on to describe the interior of the tipi:

> The internal arrangements are very simple. A round hole is dug in the centre for the fire, three sides are occupied by the beds, while the side in which is the entrance is used as kitchen, pantry, and general storeroom. The beds are elevated above the ground, perhaps from four to six inches, and serve for seats and lounges in the daytime, or when not used for sleeping purposes. They are made by laying small willow rods across a couple of poles, and covering them with buffalo skins prepared especially for the purpose.

Animal hides were used for clothing as well as bedding and tipi covers. During the summer—and sometimes well into the winter—men usually wore only breechcloths and deerskin moccasins. If the weather forced them to put on heavier clothing, often they simply wrapped a fur-lined buffalo robe around themselves. Sometimes they wore hip-high leggings and deerskin shirts as well. Women wore deerskin dresses and skirts, knee-high leggings, and moccasins. Frequently they decorated their clothing with elk teeth, bones, shells, and porcupine quills. The Kiowa dressed like most of their contemporaries on the Plains.

The Kiowa, like many other Indian peoples, believed that special spiritual powers were attached to certain substances, foods, objects, animals, songs, and rituals. In addition, certain objects could bring particularly sacred power to an individual. These articles were known as the person's "medicine." Depending on its nature, an individual's medicine could be called on to bring success in war, ensure long life, heal the sick, produce rain, or do countless other things. A person obtained his or her particular medicine either by seeking out power—such as by pledging to do the Sun Dance or going out alone to fast and pray in hope of receiving a vision—or by inheriting it from an elderly person. Upon receiving power individuals were told, perhaps during a vision, what rituals and objects were to become medicine for them and were given the ritual they would need to use in order for the medicine to become effective. The medicine might include corn, a particular stone or stick, tobacco, or paint. The rituals might include the words to a song. An individual's sacred objects were kept wrapped in a piece of deerskin or other hide container known as a medicine bundle. They were taken out of the bundle only when used to perform the medicine ceremony.

Sometimes a person's medicine was so exceptionally effective or so impor-

(continued on page 34)

Medicine Bluff, near Fort Sill in what is now the State of Oklahoma. Kiowa journeyed into this area on a vision quest. They would fast and pray in the hope of receiving a vision or their personal medicine, the songs, objects, or other symbols representing their source of spiritual power.

TANNING A HIDE

The following description of tanning an animal hide, taken from Maurice Boyd's book Kiowa Voices, *was given by Kiowa Alice Jones to Susie Peters.*

The Kiowa way of tanning a buffalo, deer, or calf hide begins almost immediately after the kill. The fresh hide is stretched and staked out on the ground. A tanning mixture is made from the liver and brains of the skinned animal. To prepare the ingredients for use, mash about one-half pound of brains and one-half pound of liver together with four tablespoons of fat. Add a small amount of water and cook the mixture slowly for an hour. Then it will be ready for use.

While the hide is staked on the ground, the cooked mixture of liver and brains is rubbed on the hide with a rag, first on one side, then on the other. With the hands and a smooth round stone, the mixture is thoroughly worked into each side of the hide. Making certain that the mixture is spread evenly over the hide, the stakes should be withdrawn from the ground and the hide rolled or folded and left overnight to allow the tanning mixture to soak in. The next day it should be washed in cold water and dried. Since this will cause it to shrink and thicken, it must be pulled and stretched back into its original shape before graining.

To grain the hide, its entire surface should be rubbed with a rough stone. Finally, the hide should be worked back and forth with a seesaw movement through a loop of rope.

The hide should then be soaked in warm water overnight. In the morning, stake it out on smooth ground, hair side down. The stakes should be driven about six inches apart and the hide stretched as tightly as possible. The hide will have pieces of flesh, fat, and tissue clinging to it. This is removed by scraping with a knife made of elk horn.

If the hide dries and hardens while you are working, wet it with warm water. When the upper surface is clean and smooth, allow it to dry and bleach in the sun for two days. The next step is to soak the hide again, then turn it over and stake it out with hair side up. The hair is scraped off in the same way as the flesh. If the hair does not come off easily, it will be necessary to resoak the hide in wood ashes and water. Mix the ashes and water in a bucket to a thick batter. Put the hide in this mixture and leave it to soak overnight. In the morning, wash out every trace of the ashes and stake it out again. The hair can now be removed easily. Allow this side to dry and bleach in the sun for two days. Then the hide is ready for use.

Stages of the tanning process are shown in this painting by 19th-century artist George Catlin. In the foreground, one woman scrapes a staked-down hide while, behind her, a second stretches another hide preparatory to the graining process. The finished product might be used in making tipis like the ones shown here.

(continued from page 31)

tant to the well-being of the tribe that it took on tribal, rather than personal, significance, and its keeper would assume a prominent position in Kiowa society. Ten medicine bundles were the most important among the Kiowa; these were known as the Ten Grandmothers. According to Kiowa belief, they had been given to the tribe by Tal-

The tai-me, *the most sacred possession of the Kiowa and central figure of their Sun Dance. It was believed to be the object through which the spiritual powers obtained in the dance were transmitted.*

lee, the supernatural child born of a union between the sun and a woman. After Tal-lee had lived on earth for a long time, he turned himself into 10 portions of medicine, which became the Ten Grandmothers.

Each Grandmother had two keepers, a man and a woman, and its own special tipi. People in physical danger could seek refuge in a tipi that housed one of the Ten Grandmothers, and their persecutors would not be allowed to enter. These bundles were so sacred that not even the keepers knew what was in them. They were opened only once a year by a religious leader, who purified them with prayer and ceremonial smoking.

The band was the basic political and economic unit in Kiowa society. Most, but not necessarily all, of the people in a band were related to each other. Band members usually lived together in a village and traveled together as they moved about on the Plains. The size of a band ranged from 12 to 50 tipis, with a family of 4 to 6 persons living in each tipi. Bands often formed around the most respected leader in a family. Membership, however, was voluntary, and it was not unusual for a man to break off from an existing band, taking with him his immediate and extended family and his friends to form another band. Bands developed out of a need for cooperation in hunting and other food-getting activities as well as for protection.

Through the years six bands emerged as the most important subdivisions within the Kiowa tribe: the *Kata*, or Biters; the *Kogui*, or Elks; the *Kaigwa*, or Kiowa proper; the *Khe-ate*, or Big Shields; the *Semat*, or Thieves (to which the Kiowa-Apache belonged); and the *Sindiyuis*, or Saynday's children. Each band was recognized as a participant in major events of the Kiowa past. Each had its own leader, and each occupied a special place in the tribe's most important ceremony, the *K'ado*, or Sun Dance.

The Sun Dance was an occasion of spiritual and national renewal. It took place once a year about the time of the summer solstice and celebrated the regeneration of life and the return of the buffalo to the Indians' hunting grounds. The Kiowa did not worship Pahy, the sun, but they held his power in awe. He was one of several spiritual forces that acted upon their world.

Shortly before the Sun Dance was to take place, the keeper of the tribe's most sacred possession, the *tai-me*, rode out to each band to announce the upcoming celebration. The tai-me was the central figure of the Sun Dance, the object through which the spiritual powers obtained through the dance were conducted. The object itself was the image of a human being carved from a small green stone. A robe of white feathers and ermine skin was draped around its shoulders, and a leaf of tobacco served as its headdress. According to Kiowa tradition, the tribe had acquired the tai-me from an Arapaho Indian, who had acquired it from a Crow leader during a Sun Dance. The Crow had given the sacred object to the Arapaho, who seemed destitute. Many of the Crow

were upset by this generosity, but they allowed the Arapaho to leave with it. In time the Arapaho prospered, and when he returned to the Crow the tai-me was stolen from him. The Arapaho was deeply saddened by the loss of the object and decided to reconstruct the image. He gave it to the Kiowa when he married a Kiowa woman. This probably occurred sometime during the mid-18th century, and the Kiowa have carefully preserved and honored the tai-me ever since.

The keeper of the tai-me, like the tai-me itself, was held in veneration by the rest of the tribe. He had inherited the honored position from a previous tai-me keeper, usually a member of the same family. His duties included calling the people together for the Sun Dance as well as conducting the religious portion of the ceremony.

Once the location and time of the dance had been announced, all the Kiowa bands congregated at the designated time and place. They camped in a huge circle, each band setting up its tipis in a specific position. Then they set to work constructing the sacred lodge in which the ceremony would be held. Ethnologist James Mooney vividly described this structure in 1898, when he was interviewed by the *Omaha Daily Bee*:

In the center of the circle stood the "medicine lodge" built for the celebration of the [sun] dance . . . This was built of cottonwood branches interwoven on seventeen poles standing in a circle around the center poles seven paces apart. Hanging to the center pole was the medicine image [tai-me], which was kept hid in a bag under strict surveillance of the priests during the year, and only brought out on the annual June festival. It was the head and shoulders of a man carved out of stone, and grotesquely painted. Above the image hung a strip of buffalo skin cut from a point a little in front of the ears to the tail. This was wrapped around a branch of cottonwood. An arbor of cottonwood boughs, which formed the secret chamber of the priests during the dance, completed the interior of the lodge.

The construction of the lodge took about six days. When it was complete the people held a buffalo dance. The dancers dressed in buffalo skins and imitated the movements and sounds of the animal. At the end of the dance the "buffalo" were driven into the ceremonial lodge. Then the young men who had pledged to do the Sun Dance entered. For four days and nights they would remain in the lodge, their eyes fixed upon the tai-me that hung from the center pole. During this time they fasted and danced in hopes of obtaining power from one of the spirit forces that guided the Kiowa's lives. Their quest could be on behalf of another person— restored health for a sick family member, for example—or on their own behalf, such as for success in war. The tai-me keeper was present throughout the entire ceremony and led the partici-

pants in the songs and rituals. After four days the pledges returned to their own tipis, where they rested and drank a beverage made from prepared roots.

While the young men were fasting inside the ceremonial lodge, the rest of the Kiowa were socializing. People greeted old friends, members of the various soldier societies gave feasts, families arranged marriages for their young people, and everyone participated in games. On the last night of the dance a big feast was held and all of the people, except those who had pledged the Sun Dance, joined in. Soon afterward the bands dispersed.

The oldest Sun Dances the Kiowa can remember took place on the northern Plains. That was in the Bighorn Mountains of Wyoming, where they probably celebrated the event with their Crow allies and their neighbors. A huge spiked circle made of boulders can still be seen there, and similar arrangements of stone, today known as "medicine wheels," are found elsewhere on the northern Plains. Although no evidence exists to demonstrate conclusively that such monuments were associated with Sun Dances, there are a few hints that this may be the case. For example, the wheel in the Bighorn Mountains appears to date back to around 1700, which would fit the Kiowa's recollections of holding the Sun Dance with the Crow in that area. Also, the medicine wheels often seem to have an emphasized spoke pointing toward the position of the rising sun on the longest day of the year, the summer solstice.

Kiowa Sun Dance *by contemporary Kiowa artist Sharron Ahtone. At the back of the lodge is a cedar screen from which eight shields hang. The tai-me is at the left of the center pole. Objects placed around the tai-me during the dance were believed to acquire the power to protect their owners from evil.*

Writes Kiowa artist James Auchiah:

With a burst of heat Pahy appeared,
Brought to us by Saynday from the
    east,
Our people saw the glory of the
    Earth—
    Maker's creation,
The visual earth spoke softly in
    nature's poetry,
And the Kiowas understood the
    power
    of the spirit force.

Thus a year in the life of the Kiowa might culminate in a Sun Dance. It would have been an eventful year that probably included a buffalo hunt, the birth of a child, a medicine man's attempt to save a grandfather, a first horse ride, and a battle with a neighboring nation. It would have been a year of tipi building and berry gathering, of movement and ritual. The 18th century on the Great Plains was a time of Kiowa cultural flowering. ▲

On the Move *by contemporary Kiowa artist Stephen Mopope.*

MIGRATIONS
1700–1833

By the beginning of the 18th century, the Kiowa controlled the area around the Black Hills of South Dakota. To the north of them lived the Cheyenne, Arapaho, and Blackfoot Indians. To the east were the Arikara, Mandan, and Hidatsa tribes, and to the west, the Shoshone and Crow. The basis of Kiowa occupation of the desirable Black Hills was threefold: They maintained a strong alliance with the largest nation to the west, the Crow; they enjoyed peaceful relations and a very successful trade relationship with Mandan, Hidatsa, and Arikara villages; and, for a time, they had no serious challenges for their territory from newcomers.

The Kiowa had first encountered the Crow as they journeyed from western Montana to the Black Hills. Around 1700, they entered into a friendly alliance with them, a shrewd diplomatic move on the part of the Kiowa. The Crow helped protect the less numerous Kiowa from enemy tribes in the region.

In the early 1700s the hunting grounds south of the Black Hills began to attract the Comanche Indians. They had left their Rocky Mountain territory and moved south of the Kiowa on land that had previously been a neutral zone noted for its heavy concentration of buffalo. The Kiowa, resenting this invasion of what they considered their hunting territory, tried to expel the Comanche from the region and drive them farther south. The Comanche, who by this time had many horses, were a formidable opponent, greatly outnumbering the Kiowa. Between 1730 and 1770 brief skirmishes occurred between the Kiowa and Comanche as hunting parties occasionally crossed each other's paths. Although no large-scale attacks took place during this period, these skirmishes led to mutual distrust, the Kiowa going so far as to name these unwelcome invaders *Gyai-ko*, or enemies. After 1770 the fighting escalated into serious warfare.

The Kiowa, however, were not solely occupied with protecting themselves from their neighbors to the south. During the same period tensions

Bear Butte, a mountain in the Black Hills of South Dakota that has religious significance for the Kiowa, Cheyenne, Sioux, and Crow, is now a registered National Natural Landmark. People of Plains Indian ancestry continue to make pilgrimages here to fast, pray, and give offerings.

between them and their northern neighbors were increasing. Their military engagements became not just a matter of defending the neutral zone to the south of their territory but, more crucially, defending their very position in the Black Hills. The Shoshone were attacking them from the west; the Cheyenne with their Arapaho allies were exerting pressure from the north; and the Sioux (Dakota), the greatest threat of all, were menacing them from the east.

The Sioux, a confederation of seven allied tribes, had obtained guns from French traders. With these weapons, which were far superior to the bows and arrows still used by most Plains Indians, the Sioux were able to wrest the northern Plains away from practically every tribe that challenged them. Their domination of this region thoroughly disrupted the Kiowa's trade with the Arikara and other agricultural tribes along the Missouri River. Eventually, the Sioux blockaded the Arikara's villages, successfully cutting off their trade with the Kiowa.

In 1781 a smallpox epidemic weakened the Kiowa's fighting strength, killing an estimated 2,000 people. With the tribe's warrior count reduced to around 300, the Kiowa were ill equipped to resist encroachment on all sides.

Near-constant harassment by the Sioux in combination with accelerated Cheyenne-Arapaho raids convinced some of the Kiowa to evacuate the Black Hills in about 1785. This decision was reached only after much deliberation and for good reason. According to Kiowa accounts, early in the tribe's history a group of warriors had decided to follow the sun south to discover where it went at the end of the summer. They traveled on horseback for many days, going farther south than any Kiowa had ever been before. One night after all but one of the warriors had fallen asleep, small men with tails appeared in the trees above. The next morning the warrior who had witnessed this amazing sight told the others about it. At first they did not believe him, but while they were preparing to leave, they had the distinct feeling they were being observed. They peered up into the branches overhead and, to their astonishment, saw the little men with tails that their comrade had described. They immediately set out for home, anxious to get away from such strange creatures. When the warriors arrived, they told their people what they had seen and counseled them against ever migrating south.

This story probably was repeated many times while the Kiowa debated whether or not to leave the Black Hills. Nevertheless, about two-thirds of the tribe decided to begin the migration that would eventually lead them to the southern Plains. But the other third, heeding the advice of their ancestors, elected to stay in the Black Hills. These people became known as the Upper Band, Northern Kiowa, or Cold Men because they remained in the north, in the colder climate. Although other Indians continued their attempts to gain possession of the Black Hills, the Northern Kiowa were at first able to maintain control of the territory. They repeatedly defeated the Shoshone and, in an effort to stifle the Sioux, made alliances with their former enemies, the Cheyenne and Arapaho, who had also been attacked by the dreaded warriors to the east. But by 1795 the Northern Kiowa, badly beaten by a major Sioux war party, close to starvation, and fearing a lasting Sioux-Cheyenne alliance, began what would be a very long migration south to rejoin the rest of the tribe on the southern Plains.

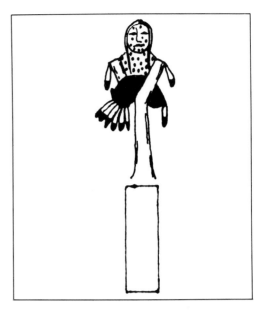

In 1781 a smallpox epidemic killed many Kiowa warriors, damaging the tribe's ability to fight off its enemies. The epidemic contributed to the Kiowa's decision to migrate to the southern Plains in 1785. This drawing records a smallpox outbreak in 1861.

Meanwhile, the Southern Kiowa were making peace with the Comanche, with whom they had maintained a running feud for several years. The Comanche themselves had been forced farther south by the Sioux. About 1790 a group of Kiowa visited a Spanish settlement in what is now New Mexico. Unknown to the Kiowa, a group of Comanche were also at the settlement. Upon discovering that their sworn enemies were but a short distance away, the two sides immediately prepared to fight. The Spanish, however, intervened, knowing that peace between these two foes would be to Spain's ben-

efit: French traders were pushing farther and farther south and west from
Canada, threatening to encroach upon
Spain's American empire. With peace
along their northern border, the Spanish could pursue anti-French activities
without having to contend with war-
ring Indian tribes.

The Kiowa and Comanche agreed to
talk. Guikate (Wolf Lying-down), the
leader of the Kiowa delegation but not
the principal chief of the tribe, said that
the Kiowa wanted peace. Pareiyi
(Afraid-of-Water), who was the Comanche leader, could not respond to
this initiative, saying he needed to con-
sult with all the Comanche on such an
important decision. He invited Guikate
to return with him to his people and
promised the Kiowa warrior that he
would be treated well. Guikate agreed

to accompany the Comanche leader
with the stipulation that his people
would return to the site of the peace
talks in one year. If at that time he could
not be found, the Kiowa would avenge
his death.

After a year of traveling with the Comanche and being treated with friendship and respect, Guikate returned to
New Mexico with his Comanche hosts.
The Kiowa and Poliakya, their principal
chief, were there to greet him and receive word of his treatment. After Guikate's favorable testimony, both sides
agreed to peace and pledged to maintain their friendship for the common
good. And thus, in 1790, the former
enemies formed a lasting alliance.

From then on the Kiowa and Comanche shared the same hunting
grounds and often went out on raids

*Map showing the route of the Lewis and Clark expedition of 1804–6, based on the original
drawings of William Clark. Near the Platte River, the explorers encountered a band of Kiowa.
Their subsequent report provided the first American description of the tribe.*

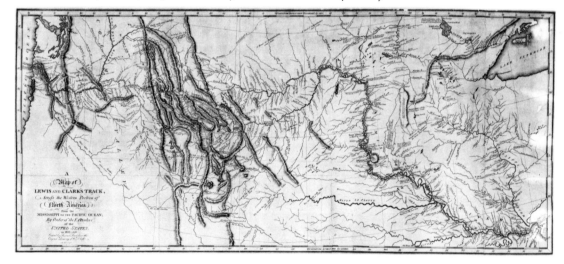

together. Their combined territory ranged from the Arkansas River in what is now western Kansas down into the Texas Panhandle, with the Kiowa staying primarily between the Arkansas and Cimarron rivers and the Comanche primarily in Texas. Together these two tribes controlled the entire southern Plains. Through the strength of their union, the Kiowa and Comanche pushed the native Mescalero and Lipan Apache Indians west and south into New Mexico and Mexico. They drove the Wichita Indians and their allies east of the Wichita Mountains of Oklahoma. And they expelled the Tonkawa Indians almost entirely from the southern edge of the Plains and into central Texas.

Even before they took command of the southern Plains, the Kiowa had been trading at Spanish settlements in New Mexico. When they could not get what they wanted by way of trade, they raided other Indians as well as European settlements along the growing frontier, taking horses, guns, and captives.

By the late 1700s, they were coming into contact with French traders as well. The French had established trading posts at St. Louis and other sites along the Mississippi River and were soon making forays westward onto the southern Plains to trade. These Spanish and French traders were probably the first non-Indians to come in contact with the Kiowa. La Salle had mentioned them in his journals as early as 1682, although he never actually met them.

He wrote that the Kiowa and Kiowa-Apache were located south of a division of the Pawnee who lived in the central Plains. They had many horses, apparently stolen from the Spanish in New Mexico. They traded these with other tribes for food and other material goods.

The earliest American description of the Kiowa is that of Meriwether Lewis and William Clark, who led the first official U.S. government expedition across the Great Plains. The explorers, who left from St. Louis in the spring of 1804, were seeking a northwest route to the Pacific Ocean as well as information on the environment of the region and the military capabilities of its inhabitants. While camped near the junction of the Missouri and Platte rivers, Lewis and Clark met Indians who spoke of the Kiowa. The explorers reported that they were told the tribe occupied 70 tipis on the North Platte River, in what is now western Nebraska, and estimated its population to be 700, approximately 200 of whom were warriors. They also reported that 300 Kiowa-Apache were living in 25 tipis farther north.

Lewis and Clark heard that the Indians were trying to get to the Missouri River to trade horses and goods of Spanish manufacture for guns and goods produced by the British. The Spanish had banned the trading of firearms, fearing that if Indians obtained guns and ammunition they would use the weapons against the Spanish in what is now New Mexico. This ban

Devils Tower, a geologic formation in eastern Wyoming, and the seven stars of the Big Dipper figure in a Kiowa legend about the stars' origin. This drawing by contemporary artist Al Momaday is from The Way to Rainy Mountain, *by N. Scott Momaday.*

caused a severe technological imbalance on the Plains, with some Indians, such as the Sioux, possessing many guns obtained from the French in Canada, while others, such as the Kiowa, owned almost none. Indians who had few contacts with French or English traders were at a decided disadvantage, being forced to fight with traditional—and far less effective—bows and arrows.

In their journals, Lewis and Clark also mentioned that the Sioux had blockaded the Arikara villages and that the Kiowa would likely migrate farther south. If their report was accurate, and there is no reason to believe it was not, then the Indians that the explorers wrote of were probably the Northern Kiowa. By 1804 the Northern Kiowa had already left their home in the Black Hills and could very possibly have been living in western Nebraska, pausing there while en route to the southern Plains. In 1805 the French trader Baptiste Lalande reported hearing that the Northern Kiowa were being prevented from reaching their relatives in New Mexico by the unrelenting menace to the east, the Sioux.

Around 1806 the Northern Kiowa were finally reunited with the Southern Kiowa. Twenty years had passed since the two groups had separated. The Southern Kiowa and their Comanche allies welcomed their kin with enthusiasm, not only because of their happiness in seeing long-absent friends and relatives but also because the Northern Kiowa would contribute to the size of the alliance. A smallpox epidemic had swept across the Plains in 1801, and, like many tribes, the Southern Kiowa had been badly affected, losing nearly half of their population to this dreaded disease.

During the first quarter of the 19th century, the Kiowa's hold on the southern Plains solidified. In 1815 they attempted to end their ongoing enmity with the Sioux, agreeing to meet with a delegation of Sioux near present-day Colorado Springs, Colorado, to discuss peace. But the talks ended in disaster, as a quarrel erupted and one of the Sioux delegates killed a Kiowa. A year later another smallpox epidemic decimated the tribe. The Kiowa's dominion over the southern Plains remained intact, however, because Indian tribes from the Red River to the Rio Grande suffered heavy losses as well.

Even after they left the region of the Black Hills, the Kiowa continued to remember their time there. They particularly revered the Devils Tower, an imposing structure of volcanic rock that pierces the eastern Wyoming landscape. An ancient Kiowa legend tells of a brother and his seven sisters. They were at play when suddenly the boy began to tremble and turned into a menacing bear. The terrified sisters fled to a giant tree stump, which began to speak, telling them to climb onto it. As the last sister reached the stump, it began to rise into the sky just ahead of the claws of the angry bear, which scored the bark of the tree. The stump bore the seven sisters into the sky, where they were transformed into the stars of the Big Dipper. To this day the Kiowa believe that their kin in the sky watch over the Kiowa dwelling on earth. The site where the sisters ascended into the heavens is Devils Tower.

Like the seven sisters who escaped the claws of their ferocious brother, the Kiowa during the late 18th century were forced to flee from their enemies on the northern Plains. The move from their homeland had not been easy, but the pressures that would face them in the decades to come would be even more threatening to their survival than those they had already overcome. ▲

Black Legs Warrior, *a painting by Roland Whitehorse, 1949.*

STRUGGLE
FOR THE
SOUTHERN PLAINS

Imkodatando Pai, "the summer that they cut off their heads," marks the opening of a perilous period in Kiowa history. It is a time of conflict, of enclosure, and of surrender. It begins with the Cut-Throat Massacre in 1833 and ends with the unconditional surrender of the Kiowa at Fort Sill in 1875. During this period, the world of the Kiowa was forever altered.

On the 1833 Kiowa calendar, the Cut-Throat Massacre is depicted by a solitary head over a black bar. That summer, at the encouragement of their principal chief, A'date (Island Man), the Kiowa had broken up into groups that were smaller than usual. This was probably because food was scarce and the chief thought that smaller, widely dispersed bands would be more successful at finding something to eat. In addition to the tribe's being more spread out than usual, many warriors had gone off on raids, leaving the camps unprotected from enemy Indians.

A'date took his own small band of followers into the Wichita Mountains to search for food. One morning a war party of Osage Indians attacked his camp, killing many of the people, including the wife of the tai-me keeper. The sacred tai-me itself was stolen. The Osage cut off the heads of the dead and placed them in kettles, leaving them at the destroyed camp for the relatives of the slain Kiowa to find. A'date escaped without being killed, but he was disgraced because of his poor judgment. He lost his position as principal chief and soon afterward was replaced by Dohasan (Little Bluff).

The following summer an expedition of U.S. soldiers led by Colonel Henry Dodge returned to the Kiowa a girl who had been captured by the Osage in the Cut-Throat Massacre. This was the first official contact between the Kiowa and the U.S. government. Dodge and his superiors in Washington, D.C., hoped to convince the Kiowa

The summer of 1833, when Osage warriors attacked and beheaded members of an isolated Kiowa camp, as recorded in the calendar of Chief Dohasan (Little Bluff).

to attend a peace council to be held at Fort Gibson, then the United States's remotest outpost on the southwestern frontier. The Kiowa responded to the government's show of good faith, and 15 of their chiefs agreed to accompany the soldiers to the fort for the meeting.

On September 2, 1834, the leaders of various southern Plains tribes gathered at Fort Gibson to discuss peace. In addition to the Kiowa, the Cherokee, Creek, Choctaw, Wichita, Waco, Comanche, and Osage were represented. The Kiowa readily embraced most of the Indian leaders as friends, but they were reluctant to make peace with the Osage.

Also present at the council was George Catlin, a self-trained artist from Philadelphia who traveled extensively among the Indians, painting their portraits and writing observations about their way of life. Over the course of the council, Catlin painted each of the Kiowa chiefs, as well as many others in attendance. He described the Kiowa as being "tall and erect, with an easy and graceful gait—with long hair, cultivated oftentimes so as to reach nearly to the ground."

The peace talks of 1834 paved the way for a formal peace treaty between the southern Plains tribes in 1835. Most of the Indians pledged to live in peace and friendship with each other as well as with citizens of the United States. They agreed to share a common hunting territory and to allow U.S. citizens safe passage through this territory. Furthermore, they promised to pursue peaceful relations with Mexico and other nations with which they were then on unfriendly terms.

The Kiowa, however, objected to some terms of the treaty and left the council early without signing it. Later that year they reached an agreement with the Osage for the return of the tai-me, and in June of 1836 they held the first Sun Dance since the tai-me was stolen in 1833. But the U.S. government was not satisfied with this informal agreement between the two Indian nations; they wanted the Kiowa to sign a formal treaty similar to the one accepted by the other Plains Indians in 1835. In an effort to convince the tribe to enter into such an agreement, government officials plied the Kiowa leaders with presents and trade goods. Eventually their efforts paid off. In the spring of 1837, ten Kiowa chiefs, among them Takatacouche (Black Bird), Sensondacat (White Bird), and Kehimhi (Prairie Dog), met with government officials at Fort Gibson and signed their first treaty with the United States. But Dohasan, the principal chief, did not sign the treaty. His reasons are not known, but he may have believed that such an agreement was not in the Kiowa's best interests.

Like the 1835 treaty, this one emphasized peace between the Indians and the United States. Injuries suffered by the citizens of each nation at the hands of the other were forgiven. In addition, Kiowa hunting rights were recognized throughout the southern Plains and safe passage through Kiowa territory was guaranteed for U.S. citizens. The Kiowa also agreed to seek peace with Mexico and other nations with whom they were on hostile terms. Although these "other nations" were not specifically mentioned, the U.S. government implied that it wanted the

Kiowa to end their violent feuds with the Dakota and Pawnee, as well as with non-Indians in the Republic of Texas.

From the time the first settlers in what would eventually become Texas began establishing farms on the Indians' hunting territory, the Kiowa and their Comanche allies resisted these unwelcome intruders. The settlers saw their increasing advances into the frontier as the conquest of their land; the Indians saw them as trespassing and were determined to expel the homesteaders: If the settlers would not leave peaceably, then the Indians would have to force them out. It was not long before the two sides were at war, each seeking

Portrait of Chief Dohasan by George Catlin. Dohasan came to power after the 1833 Cut-throat Massacre and served the Kiowa as principal chief for more than 30 years.

to retaliate for offenses committed by the other. As long as settlers threatened to destroy the open range—and with it the buffalo—the Kiowa would not make peace.

Besides, the Kiowa did not consider Texans to be U.S. citizens anyway. And, until 1845—the year Texas was admitted to the United States—they were not, even though many who settled there had been residents of the United States before moving to Mexican-held Texas. So the Kiowa continued to raid farmsteads in Texas, and the hatred between the two enemies continued to grow.

Nevertheless, with official promises of peace, U.S. traders were quick to establish themselves on the southern Plains. Shortly after the treaties of 1837 were signed, Auguste P. Chouteau, a seasoned trader and prominent citizen of St. Louis, opened the first post in Kiowa territory along Cache Creek, in what is now southwestern Oklahoma. Chouteau had been present at all the treaty councils held at Fort Gibson. As a result, he immediately understood the significance of the treaties. With the threat of attack by Indians no longer a major concern, he could now set up permanent posts in a region that had previously been impenetrable. The post was closed in 1838 after Chouteau's death, but it was soon followed by others.

In the 1830s the Bent brothers, William and Charles, built a trading post in Cheyenne territory, along the Arkansas River near what is now Las An-

Bent's Fort, in an 1845 drawing by J. W. Abert. The brothers William and Charles Bent established a trading post along the Arkansas River in the 1830s. It soon became the trading center of the Santa Fe Trail, serving both white settlers and Indians.

imas, Colorado. For many years this post, known as Bent's Fort, would be the center of trade along the Santa Fe Trail, the main overland route through the West. Beginning in 1840 the Kiowa regularly visited the fort as well as others established by the Bents. There they traded horses, buffalo robes, and hides for metal utensils, cloth, woven blankets, and other material goods they desired.

Prior to 1840 an ongoing war with the Cheyenne had prevented the Kiowa from trading at Bent's Fort. In 1840, however, the two sides made peace, establishing the Arkansas River as the boundary between them but agreeing to share their hunting grounds. This pact created a formidable alliance that included the Kiowa-Apache, Comanche, and Arapaho, and it intensified the force with which the southern Plains Indians could combat non-Indians' increasing encroachment onto their land. The added warrior strength was especially important because a smallpox epidemic had raced through the Kiowa camps during the winter of 1839–40. It has been estimated that one-third of the Plains Indian population died during this particular epidemic. Some tribespeople fled to the Staked Plain of the Texas Panhandle to try to escape the disease.

A few years later non-Indian settlers introduced a new disease, cholera. In 1849 more than half of the tribespeople perished in the first major cholera epidemic. Many committed suicide in order to avoid the dreaded disease. The

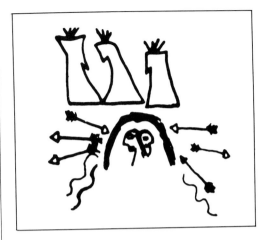

This drawing, from Chief Dohasan's calendar of Kiowa history, represents a Cheyenne attack on the tribe in the summer of 1838. Within two years, however, the two tribes formed an alliance to resist non-Indian settlers.

survivors remembered this epidemic as a greater catastrophe than any of the earlier smallpox epidemics.

But an even greater threat to the Plains Indians' survival was beginning to emerge: The buffalo herds were declining. Several factors contributed to this disaster. Homesteaders plowed up the grasslands to establish their farms, destroying the buffalo's food supply. In addition, non-Indian hunters recklessly slaughtered thousands of buffalo for sport, leaving the carcasses to rot. Finally, the Indians themselves overhunted the buffalo in order to obtain more hides to exchange for trade goods.

The Kiowa calendar records the impact of the declining buffalo population on the Indians' way of life. In 1841, illustrated on a Kiowa calendar as "the

Kiowa hide painting of an intertribal treaty negotiation. By the late 1840s, relations among various tribes who had signed peace agreements a decade earlier were growing strained, as Plains Indians differed about how to deal with encroaching homesteaders.

summer the Pawnees were massacred on the South Canadian river," the annual Sun Dance could not be held because of the scarcity of buffalo. During the "antelope-driving winter" of 1848, the Kiowa had to hunt antelope because their reserves of buffalo meat had been consumed and the people were starving. As the buffalo herds dwindled, entries depicting such events appeared more and more frequently.

As the buffalo herds decreased, tensions between the southern Plains In-

dians and non-Indians increased. Kiowa raids into Mexico and Texas continued, mostly due to the need for food. The tribe lost several of its leading chiefs, among them Adalhabakia, Crow Neck, Giadeete, and War Bonnet, in various skirmishes. In their place emerged younger, even more aggressive leaders.

During the 1840s tensions occurred within the Kiowa-Comanche alliance as well. The Kiowa calendar for the year 1847 depicts the death of the Comanche chief Mankaguadal (Red Sleeve). He had called the Kiowa cowards for refusing to raid U.S. citizens and thereby break the treaty of 1837. After being shot in an attack against traders traveling the Santa Fe Trail, he sent a message to the Kiowa begging them to rescue him. The Kiowa refused, having been insulted by Red Sleeve's taunts of cowardice, and the Comanche leader was left to die.

Even though the Kiowa honored the treaty of 1837, their raids into Texas after 1845 were technically violations of the agreement: In that year Texas became part of the United States, and its residents became U.S. citizens. The following year the United States declared war on Mexico. With the close of the war in 1848, the victorious U.S. government acquired New Mexico, another region often subjected to Kiowa raids in the past. With each acquisition, the distinction between Americans, Texans, and Mexicans evaporated, and the Kiowa diplomacy had to adjust.

Although by the middle of the 19th century the Kiowa still owned few guns, they remained a formidable fighting force. Their outstanding skills as archers and lancers, as well as their extraordinary horsemanship, made them a very real threat to the expanding American frontier. During the 1850s the U.S. government built a series of military forts along the Texas frontier, among them Fort Graham, Fort Worth, Fort Belknap, and Fort Arbuckle. However, the forts were too far apart to prevent Indian raids into Texas.

Detail from painting on the tipi of Chief Dohasan. Although the Kiowa had relatively few firearms (unlike, for example, the Sioux), they ably defended their territory in clashes with the U.S. military.

The U.S. Army also had trouble quelling Indian raids along the Santa Fe Trail, which linked Independence, Missouri, and Santa Fe, New Mexico. Each year almost $2 million in merchandise was transported in both directions over this route, much of it across unsettled wilderness that would later become the states of Kansas and Colorado. The wagon trains were prime targets for attack by Indians as well as non-Indians, and a successful wagon raid could yield a booty of desirable trade goods or hides.

In 1853, after military efforts proved inadequate to protect the Texas frontier and the Santa Fe Trail, the U.S. government decided to use diplomatic measures. Thomas Fitzpatrick was appointed the federal representative or agent designated to manage relations

Setangya (Sitting Bear), a Kiowa band chief and prominent warrior. His signature on the Treaty of Fort Atkinson in 1853 promised peaceful relations with the United States in exchange for cash and trade goods; however, the tribe continued raids into Mexico and Texas, to the chagrin of U.S. officials.

with the various southern Plains tribes. In July of that year he gathered the Kiowa, Kiowa-Apache, and Comanche together at Fort Atkinson, near what is now Davis, Oklahoma, for a treaty council. Here some of the lesser tribal leaders signed the Treaty of Fort Atkinson. They agreed to maintain peace with Mexico as well as the United States. Although no official representatives of Mexico attended the council, the United States, having only recently won the Mexican War, was anxious to prevent further hostilities that might re-

open the fighting. Because the Indians were dependent on the proceeds of their raids into Mexico, the tribal leaders were reluctant to agree to these terms. Eventually, Setangya (Sitting Bear), a band chief and prominent warrior, signed the treaty for the Kiowa. In addition to promises of peaceful relations, the Indians agreed to stop attacking wagon trains along the Santa Fe Trail and to allow the U.S. government to build military forts and roads through their territory. In return the federal government would pay the three allied tribes a combination of cash and trade goods totaling $18,000 a year for a period of 10 years.

The Kiowa calendar does not note the Treaty of Fort Atkinson, nor does the name of Principal Chief Dohasan appear on the agreement. In all probability the Kiowa chiefs never officially discussed the treaty, and the Kiowa may not have been officially represented in the treaty party. In any event, the Indians continued their raids into Texas and Mexico, leading one exasperated government official to declare, "Nothing short of a thorough chastisement, which they [the Kiowa and Comanche] so richly deserve, will bring these people to their proper senses."

Not all of the Kiowa's raids were carried out against non-Indians, however. During the summer of 1854 a war party of 1,500 Kiowas, Comanches, Cheyennes, and Arapahos attacked a group of Sac and Fox Indians camped in the Smoky Hills in eastern Kansas Territory. The Sac and Fox had been removed to Kansas Territory from their homelands in Illinois after an unsuccessful war with the U.S. Army. With the shortage of food becoming an increasing problem, the Kiowa and their allies hoped to drive these newcomers out of the southern Plains. The battle was a disaster, however. Equipped with government-issued rifles, the Sac and Fox, who had only 100 warriors, easily defeated their attackers, who carried only bows and arrows. It was a crushing defeat for the Kiowa and an ominous portent of things to come.

Year by year the frontier intruded farther into Kiowa territory, and year by year the Kiowa's frustrations grew. Increasingly their buffalo hunts ended in failure; often they had to resort to eating jackrabbit meat or wild plant foods. Sometimes they ate nothing at all. In 1858 thousands of gold miners rushed through the heart of Kiowa territory on their way to Pike's Peak in the Rocky Mountains. Many stayed on to build scattered villages and ranches on territory that, according to treaties, belonged to the Plains Indians. In protest, the Kiowa could only resort to violence. When in the late 1850s the Indian agent threatened to cut off their treaty payments and send the U.S. Army after them if they did not cease their hostilities, Principal Chief Dohasen retorted:

> The white chief is a fool. He is a coward. His heart is small—not larger than a pebble stone. His men are not strong—too few to contend with my warriors. . . . There are three chiefs—the white chief, the Spanish chief, and myself. The Spanish chief and myself are men. We do bad to each other sometimes, stealing horses and taking scalps, but we do not get mad and act the fool. The white chief is a child, and like a child gets mad quick. When my young men, to keep their women and children from starving, take from the white man passing through our country, killing and driving away the buffalo, a cup of sugar or coffee, the white chief is angry and threatens to send his soldiers. I have looked for them a long time, but they have not come.

Eventually the soldiers did come. In 1860 a joint force of Texas Rangers and Tonkawa, Wichita, and Caddo Indians surprised a group of Comanche and Kiowa warriors camped just south of the Arkansas River in what is now western Oklahoma. An important Kiowa warrior, Bird Rising, was killed in the battle. The following year the Kiowa retaliated, killing many of the Tonkawa who had participated in the raid and sending the rest fleeing back into central Texas.

Between 1861 and 1865 the threat of direct military attacks on the Kiowa decreased as U.S. soldiers were needed to fight in the Civil War. But the crisis between North and South did not entirely halt the fighting between the Indians and the settlers. In Colorado Territory, Governor John Evans responded to public pressure by encouraging a campaign of extermination against the Indians in the territory. He instructed the

Colorado militia to fire on Indians not in their designated areas—and even on those who were. In the fall of 1864 a band of friendly Cheyenne under Black Kettle was camped along Sand Creek in southeastern Colorado Territory. The Indians had been promised the protection of the nearby garrison at Fort Lyon, and most of their warriors were away hunting buffalo. On November 29, the Colorado militia under the command of Colonel John Chivington opened fire on the camp. Two-thirds of the roughly 600 Indians were women and children. At Black Kettle's tipi an American flag fluttered prominently. Government officials had told the Cheyenne chief that as long as the American flag flew over him, he and his people would not be harmed by U.S. soldiers. Chivington and the Colorado militia, however, ignored the flag, as well as the white flag of truce that Black Kettle hastily raised below it. They killed indiscriminately— young and old, men, women, and children, sparing no one, not even the children of non-Indian traders and their Indian wives. And the soldiers were not content merely to kill their victims. The bodies of the slain were viciously mutilated, sometimes beyond recognition. Even though many in the camp escaped, more than 100 people were slaughtered.

Word of the Sand Creek Massacre spread like wildfire over the Plains. It was quickly becoming apparent to the Kiowa and other Plains Indians that the United States did not differentiate between friendly and unfriendly Indians.

All too often, they discovered, an Indian tribe that agreed to peace faced defeat and probable extermination; fighting a war at least allowed for an honorable death.

At about the same time as the Sand Creek Massacre, Kit Carson, a noted trapper and scout, led a raid on the Kiowa and Comanche who were camped for the winter near Adobe Walls, an abandoned trading post in the Texas Panhandle. He attacked the first camp he came to, which happened to be that of Principal Chief Dohasan. At the first sound of gunfire many of the Indians fled downstream to warn the other camps that soldiers were coming. Carson pursued them until a force of warriors arrived from downstream camps and counterattacked his troops. Throughout the day the warriors held the soldiers off. Finally Carson ordered his men to retreat. As the soldiers made their way back to their base, they passed again through the camp they had attacked, burning all the Indians' lodges as well as their possessions and supplies of dried meat. In all 176 tipis were destroyed, and many of the people were left without clothing or food at the onset of winter.

Despite these acts of hostility, the Kiowa agreed to attend another peace council with the U.S. government in October 1865. It was held at the mouth of the Little Arkansas River near what is now Wichita, Kansas, and included representatives of the Kiowa, Kiowa-Apache, Comanche, Cheyenne, and Arapaho tribes. Unlike the Treaty of

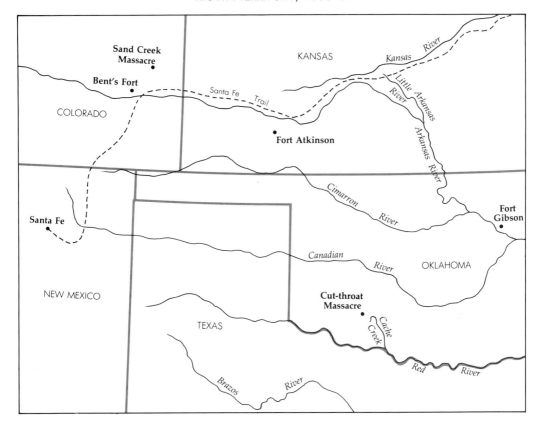

Fort Atkinson, all of the Kiowa's leading chiefs were present at the council and all signed the treaty. The terms of the agreement were drastic: Gone were the days of equal military strength and hence treaties of mutual respect. The Indians agreed to relinquish all claims to the southern Plains; they would live on government-held land in western Indian Territory (later Oklahoma) and Texas and remain within the boundaries of this reservation, which were as yet undetermined. They had to release all non-Indian prisoners taken captive over the years and to cease all hostilities against non-Indians—especially those traveling the Santa Fe Trail. But before signing the treaty, Principal Chief Dohasan protested being confined to a reservation and commented that Kiowa country ran from Fort Laramie in Colorado Territory to the Rio Grande. Along with his signature on the document appear those of Tene-angop'te (Kicking Bird), Gui-pago (Lone Wolf), Satanta (White Bear), and Setimkia (Stumbling Bear).

Dohasan died on the reservation near the Cimarron River shortly after signing the Little Arkansas Treaty. For

Setimkia (Stumbling Bear), a Kiowa band chief and one of several signers of the Little Arkansas Treaty of 1865, a turning point for the Kiowa. In it, the chiefs agreed—under protest—to confine their tribe to a reservation.

Almost from the beginning neither the Indians nor the United States honored the terms of the Little Arkansas Treaty. Thousands of settlers established farms on the Kiowa's reservation. At the same time, Kiowa raids into Texas continued.

In the fall of 1867 the United States again tried to make peace with the Indians. In October a six-member peace commission met with representatives of the Kiowa, Comanche, Kiowa-Apache, Cheyenne, and Arapaho tribes at Medicine Lodge Creek, 60 miles south of Fort Larned, Kansas. More than 4,000 Indians gathered to witness the proceedings. Because the commission's primary interpreter spoke only Comanche, it is probable that many of the Indians did not understand the full impact of the treaty. Nevertheless, some leaders of all the tribes signed, agreeing to share a reservation between the Canadian and Red rivers in southwestern Indian Territory. Within these boundaries the Kiowa, Kiowa-Apache, and Comanche were to remain between the Washita River on the north and the Red River and its North Fork on the south and west. In addition, the Indians were to allow the construction of a railroad through their territory and to farm the land that the government provided. For its part, the government would give the Indians farm equipment and cattle as well as clothing and other trade goods.

At first the Kiowa chief Satanta, noted throughout the Plains for his gift of oratory, was reluctant to sign the

more than 30 years he had served his tribe as principal chief and had watched as the United States annexed the Kiowa's homelands, eventually bringing an end to Kiowa life as he had known it. He had been the unifying force within the tribe. After his death in 1866, he was succeeded as principal chief by Lone Wolf, who shared power with Satanta and Kicking Bird. Some of the tribespeople favored Kicking Bird, who advocated peaceful relations with the United States. Others rallied around Lone Wolf and Satanta, the primary supporters of forceful resistance.

treaty. "All the land south of the Arkansas [River] belongs to the Kiowa and Comanche," he said, "and I don't want to give any of it away."

> I love the land[,] the buffalo and will not part with it. . . . I have heard that you intend to settle us on a reservation near the mountains. I don't want to settle. I love to roam over the prairies. There I feel free and happy, but when we settle down we grow pale and die. . . . A long time ago this land belonged to our fathers; but when I go up to the river I see camps of soldiers. . . . These soldiers cut down my timber, they kill my buffalo; when I see that, my heart feels like bursting; I feel sorry.

Eventually 10 Kiowa chiefs, including Satanta, Kicking Bird, and Setangya, signed the Treaty of Medicine Lodge Creek. Lone Wolf, who did not trust the United States to keep its word, refused to sign. As a last-minute concession, the U.S. government decided to allow the Kiowa and Comanche to continue to hunt on their former lands in western Kansas and Texas.

Shortly after the treaty council at Medicine Lodge Creek, the Kiowa left to hunt buffalo in the Texas Panhandle. But by this time the herds had been greatly depleted, and the Indians returned home with little to feed their families. They approached the Indian agent at Fort Cobb to demand the provisions that had been promised them in the recent treaty. But Congress had not yet approved the treaty, and the agent

had nothing to distribute. This news did not sit well with the Kiowa and, in their desperation to obtain the food they needed, they raided the nearby Wichita and Caddo tribes.

It was not long before the Kiowa were carrying out raids in Texas again. The Indian agent at Fort Cobb, William B. Hazen, warned the Kiowa that if they did not stop, American soldiers would be sent out to punish them. In the meantime, the Cheyenne and Arapaho continued to seek revenge for the Sand Creek Massacre by attacking U.S. citizens in Kansas and eastern Colorado. In response General Philip Sheridan, the senior army official in charge of the southern Plains, planned a winter cam-

The death of Principal Chief Dohasan in 1866, as recorded in a Kiowa calendar. The owl symbolizes death. The wagon identifies Dohasan; the U.S. government had given him such a wagon many years earlier.

paign against the Cheyenne, Kiowa, and others. He reasoned that in winter "their ponies would be thin, and weak from lack of food, and in the cold and snow, without strong ponies to transport their villages and plunder," they could easily be overtaken by his troops.

Sheridan's plans involved a three-pronged invasion of the Canadian and Washita river valleys, where the Indians were camped for the winter. A column of soldiers under Major Andrew W. Evans was to march eastward from Fort Bascom, New Mexico; another column under Major Eugene A. Carr was to march southeastward from Fort Lyon, Colorado; a third column under Colonel George Armstrong Custer was to push southward from Fort Larned, Kansas.

On the morning of November 27, 1868, Custer's soldiers reached the first Indian camp, which was situated along the Washita River in what is now southwestern Oklahoma. It was a foggy morning and the snow was deep. The Indians had no warning of the impending attack. The soldiers opened fire on the sleeping camp, which happened to be that of Black Kettle, the Cheyenne chief whose village had been destroyed at Sand Creek. As the startled Indians attempted to flee, they were cut down by the soldiers' bullets. Black Kettle and his wife were shot from their pony as they tried to cross the Washita River. The entire attack lasted only a few minutes. One hundred and three Indians had been killed and 53 women and children captured.

Custer's soldiers then proceeded in the direction of the next camp, but they were held off by a force of warriors who had been alerted by the sound of gun-

The U.S.-Indian peace council at Medicine Lodge Creek, Kansas, as depicted in the November 16, 1874, issue of Harper's Weekly. *The Kiowa, Comanche, Kiowa-Apache, Cheyenne, and Arapaho tribes all participated.*

shots from the initial invasion. At the end of the day the soldiers retreated, and the Battle of the Washita was over.

If the southern Plains Indians had so far doubted the United States's threats of punitive military measures, Sheridan's winter campaign of 1868–69 erased any lingering disbelief. The message to the Indians was now painfully clear: Cease all fighting or else face annihilation. The government promised the Indians rations of food and an end to the killings if they settled near the military forts on their reservations.

Most of the Kiowa eventually gathered at Fort Cobb, forced into submission more by an act of trickery than by the army's promises of peace and food. Shortly after the Battle of the Washita, Satanta and Lone Wolf had delivered a message from Agent Hazen to Colonel Custer informing him that the Kiowa had not taken part in the battle. The two war chiefs, who were carrying a white flag of truce, were immediately seized. The rest of the Kiowa fled upon hearing of the capture of their chiefs and the approach of a column of troops. Army officials threatened to hang Satanta and Lone Wolf the following day unless the Kiowa gathered at Fort Cobb. Most of the bands arrived by the appointed hour, and the chiefs' lives were spared.

But in the spring of 1871, the Kiowa warriors had grown so perturbed over the lack of rations and the white men's senseless killing of the buffalo that many pressed for a retaliatory raid into Texas. In mid-May a large war party of Kiowa and Comanche attacked a wagon train traveling the Butterfield Overland Mail Company's route through central Texas. On the advice of their medicine man, Mamante, the warriors had remained hidden and allowed an earlier caravan to pass without harm. Although the Indians did not know it, this train was carrying General William Tecumseh Sherman, commander of the U.S. Army. The war party waited for the larger caravan that Mamante promised would follow, and Sherman was spared almost certain death. A short time later 10 wagons appeared. In the skirmish that ensued seven teamsters were killed and five escaped. General Sherman was outraged when he learned of the ambush and determined to punish the offenders.

When the Kiowa returned to the agency to receive rations, Satanta boldly admitted to leading the attack. "Yes, I led in that raid," he said. "I have repeatedly asked for arms and ammunition, which have not been furnished. I have made many other requests which have not been granted. You do not listen to my talk." He went on to name Setangya, Big Tree, and several other chiefs as accomplices.

As it happened, General Sherman was visiting the agency that day. The chiefs were introduced to Sherman, and Satanta again admitted to leading the raid. Sherman ordered that Satanta, Setangya, and Big Tree be arrested on the spot and sent to Texas to stand trial for the crime. A few days later the three chiefs, handcuffed and riding in heavily

Setangya's Death Song *by Ernie Keahbone.*

guarded wagons, began their journey to Texas. They had only gone a short distance when Setangya started singing the death song of the Koitsenko warrior society to which he belonged:

> Even if I survive, I will not live
> forever,
> Only the Earth remains forever;
> Even if I survive, I will not live
> forever,
> Only the sun remains forever.

As he sang he managed to work his hands out of the manacles. Then, taking a small knife that he had concealed under his blanket, he stabbed one of his guards in the leg. A soldier in the next wagon immediately fired upon the elderly chief, who died alongside the road where his captors dumped him.

The two other Kiowa chiefs proceeded to Texas, where they were found guilty of murder and sentenced to be hung. Public outcry at the army's brutal treatment of the Indians—as well as Satanta's warning that if both he and Big Tree were hanged even more blood would be shed—persuaded Texas governor Edmund J. Davis to commute the sentences to life imprisonment. The two Kiowa war chiefs were jailed at the Huntsville State Prison, where they were put to work laying a railroad line.

When Setangya sang his death song, he sang not only for himself but for the traditional Kiowa way of life as well. Gone were the days of the endless prairies and the days of Kiowa supremacy over the southern Plains. With Setangya dead and Satanta and Big Tree jailed, only Lone Wolf remained to carry on the fight to preserve the Indians' old ways. In 1872 the people selected him to head a delegation of Kiowa leaders that had been invited to meet with the commissioner of Indian affairs in Washington, D.C. Lone Wolf refused to attend the meeting until he consulted with Satanta and Big Tree, who, though jailed, were still considered to be the primary chiefs of the Kiowa. With much trepidation, U.S. officials agreed to transport the two leaders to St. Louis to meet with Lone Wolf. There the three war chiefs devised a plan that would lead to the prisoners' release.

Once in Washington, Lone Wolf was presented with an ultimatum: He could settle his people within 10 miles of the agency by December 15 and cease raiding in Texas or risk being killed by U.S. soldiers instructed to shoot any Indians who went outside of the designated location. Lone Wolf refused to comply. As long as Satanta and Big Tree remained in a Texas prison, Lone Wolf said, his men would continue to fight the Texans. By holding to this condition, Lone Wolf secured the promise that the two chiefs would be released if his warriors exhibited good behavior for the next six months.

Lone Wolf, who became the Kiowa's leader following the death of Setangya and the imprisonment of Satanta and Big Tree.

In the spring of 1873 Satanta and Big Tree were released, contingent upon the Kiowa's continuing good behavior. They both knew that the Kiowa ways of the past would soon be altered. According to Old Lady Horse, a renowned Kiowa storyteller, the buffalo saw that their day was done. They had left the Plains and gone to live inside Mount Scott, the sacred mountain on the Kiowa reservation in Oklahoma. But even though the buffalo were gone, the Kiowa nation remained. They had survived. But before they could reclaim their cultural heritage in the 20th century, they would have to endure the indignity of being forced to reject their own culture for that of their conquerors. This process is known as assimilation. ▲

Kiowa Flute Dancer, *a 1933 watercolor by Stephen Mopope.*

ASSIMILATION AND RESISTANCE 1875–1906

The next four decades were filled with attempts by the U.S. government to destroy the culture of the Kiowa and all other Indians. It was a time of tremendous suffering for the Kiowa, but it was also an era when the Kiowa nation survived the transition from the values of their Plains culture to modern Native American values.

The policy of the federal government was straightforward: Destroy the Indian in the Indian. To accomplish this goal, the Departments of War and Interior sought to alter fundamental Kiowa culture by attacking Kiowa religion, family life, economic activities, and leadership.

In 1869 the U.S. government initiated a new peace policy toward American Indians, known informally as the "Quaker Policy." Under newly elected president Ulysses S. Grant, members of the Society of Friends (Quaker) and other Christian faiths were appointed as Indian agents. It was hoped that these advocates of Christianity and peace would be particularly effective in convincing the Indians to embrace the ways of non-Indian society. The reformers energetically implemented a campaign to teach the Indians to read and write English, to force them to become farmers rather than hunters, and to immerse them in the beliefs of Christianity.

The first Kiowa-Comanche agent was Lawrie Tatum, a Quaker and an Iowa farmer. He tried to bring about cultural change by withholding rations, prohibiting the use of tobacco, and giving extra rations of sugar, coffee, and other desirable goods to those who behaved well. Nevertheless, his efforts failed to sway the Kiowa from their traditional ways. The men scoffed at the idea of farming, which was customarily women's work in most Indian communities, and they continued to range into Texas to hunt buffalo and raid farmsteads.

When Agent Lawrie Tatum learned of the return of the Kiowa's leading war

Chief Kicking Bird, who was forced in 1875 to choose 26 Kiowa warriors to be imprisoned at Fort Marion, Florida, as part of the federal government's reprisal against Indian resistance. He died shortly afterward, possibly poisoned by a fellow Kiowa.

chiefs from Texas, he resigned. By this time the devout Quaker had become convinced that the only way to subdue the Kiowa was with military force; the return of the chiefs only guaranteed more bloodshed. No longer an advocate of nonviolence, Tatum called for troops to solve the Kiowa problem.

Upon Satanta's release from prison he gave away his sacred medicine lance and shield and vowed to give up the warpath forever. But he could not stop the younger warriors of the tribe from raiding. The agency still failed to provide the Kiowa with adequate rations of food, and the warriors were forced to look elsewhere to find them. In June 1874 a group of Kiowa, Comanche, and Cheyenne Indians attacked a party of non-Indian buffalo hunters at Adobe Walls, a trading post in the Texas Panhandle. The hunters, who had powerful rifles, killed many warriors and held off the Indians. The war party conceded defeat and broke up into small groups on the Staked Plains.

Shortly after the incident at Adobe Walls, Satanta was rearrested. He maintained that he had not taken part in the raid, but he was nevertheless held accountable for the actions of his warriors. He was returned to prison in Texas, where he died several years later.

Infuriated by the continuing attacks on U.S. citizens, the army resumed its pursuit of Indians with renewed vigor. In September 1874 a column of soldiers under Ronald Mackenzie opened fire on a joint Kiowa, Comanche, and Cheyenne camp in the Palo Duro Canyon in the Texas Panhandle. Although they killed only three Indians, the soldiers struck a decisive blow, destroying the entire village, including the Indians' food, clothing, and horses. With winter coming on and nothing to sustain them, most of the Kiowa drifted back to the agency at Fort Sill. By April 1875 all of the Indians had surrendered, and the war for the southern Plains was over.

The Kiowa reluctantly settled down to reservation life. Most settled in the northern part of the reserve around Mount Scott and the Washita River, away from the agency at Fort Sill. In an effort to convince the Indians to adopt non-Indian ways, the government built 10 houses for the tribe's prominent chiefs and provided them with furniture and other household items. Most of the chiefs, however, preferred to live in their tipis, and it was only after the Indian agent enticed them with gifts of trade goods that the leaders agreed to move into the houses. But after a few years not even offers of trade goods could keep them there, and the chiefs went back to using their tipis. By 1886 one of the houses had burned down, and only nine were left on the entire Kiowa-Comanche reservation, including the Fort Sill area.

The Indian agents also had trouble inducing Kiowa men to take up farming. They provided plows, seed, and advice, but lack of interest, and more important, lack of rainfall and tillable land, doomed the government's efforts. Later the agents supplied the Kiowa with cattle in the hopes of convincing them to take up ranching, which was more suited to the southwestern Oklahoma terrain, but again the Indians wanted no part of it.

Although the Kiowa continued to hunt to sustain themselves and their families, by the late 1870s the buffalo had almost completely vanished from

Kiowa Submission to the Agency *by contemporary Kiowa artist Robert Redbird shows the aftermath of the destruction of the Kiowa-Comanche-Cheyenne camp in Palo Duro Canyon, Texas, in 1874 by the U.S. Army. The Indians were forced to return to the reservation and virtually ceased resisting U.S. policies.*

the southern Plains. In 1879 a Kiowa who was escorting a detachment of U.S. soldiers was murdered and scalped by Texas Rangers while hunting buffalo off the reservation. (The Rangers were an important quasi-military and law enforcement institution left over from the days when Texas was an independent republic.) In retaliation a war party of Kiowa attacked and killed a Texas civilian. Soon afterward Congress passed legislation making it illegal for any Kiowa to leave the reservation. This law, along with the disappearance of the buffalo, effectively put an end to the Kiowa's former way of life.

Confined to the reservation, the Kiowa were subjected even more to the forced assimilation of the government's "civilization" program. Because most of the people lived in the northern part of the reservation, the agency was moved to the town of Anadarko, on the Wash-

ita River, which was nearer to the Kiowa settlements. Guided by the belief that the Indians should be making attempts to feed themselves—and acting in response to allegations of overspending by the Department of the Interior, which supervised Indian matters through the Bureau of Indian Affairs (BIA)—the BIA reduced the Kiowa's rations to dangerously low levels. At one point Agent P. B. Hunt could offer the starving Kiowa and Comanche nations nothing but coffee. Finally, government officials approved emergency funds to purchase much-needed beef.

In the 1880s neighboring ranchers and farmers eager to own the Indians' land began pressing for the opening of the Kiowa-Comanche reservation to non-Indian settlement. Some ranchers illegally placed their stock on the Indians' land and tried to steal the Indians' horses. Eventually the ranchers ap-

Kiowa await the issuing of rations at the agency headquarters in Anadarko, Indian Territory, in 1892.

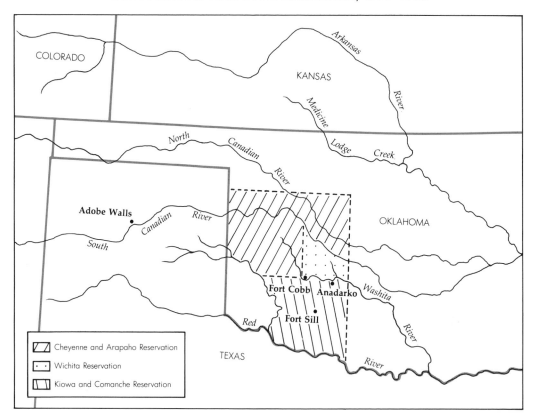

COLORADO

Arkansas

KANSAS

River

North

Medicine

Canadian

Lodge

Creek

River

Adobe Walls

Canadian

River

OKLAHOMA

South

Fort Cobb

Anadarko

Washita

Red

Fort Sill

River

TEXAS

River

Cheyenne and Arapaho Reservation

Wichita Reservation

Kiowa and Comanche Reservation

proached the Kiowa and Comanche about leasing parts of the reservation. Although many of the Comanche agreed to this proposition, the Kiowa resisted, wary of relinquishing any of their land, even if only temporarily. The federal government then ruled that the land could be leased and stipulated a grass payment, or leasing fee, of $9.50 a year. Most Kiowa still refused to lease their land.

Meanwhile, a subtle assault on Kiowa customs was in progress. Kiowa children were reluctant to attend schools, and their parents did not see value in the whites' system of educa-

tion. Agents enticed the children to attend day schools on the reservation by giving them food and promising them money. When these methods did not work children were captured or rations due their families withheld until the children were given over to the agent and forced to attend schools.

Some Kiowa children were sent away to boarding schools off the reservation, usually quite far away. Here their hair was cut, and they were given non-Indian clothing. The wearing of Indian clothing was banned, as was the use of the Kiowa language and any traditional Indian religious practices. Es-

The Oak Creek Sun Dance of the summer of 1887, as recorded in a Kiowa calendar. This was the last Kiowa Sun Dance because this observance, long opposed by Christian missionaries, was prohibited by the U.S. government later that year.

sentially the focus of these schools was to teach Indian children how to be non-Indians: Boys learned to farm and girls learned homemaking and secretarial skills. During their stay at the school, which could range from three to five years, the students were not allowed to see their parents. By removing the Indians from their familiar surroundings, the government hoped they would more readily assimilate, that is, take on the ways of non-Indian culture.

Conditions at schools both on and off the reservation were at best bleak. One BIA inspector described the agency school on the Kiowa-Comanche reservation as an "asylum," a comparison to the horrendous conditions in the institutions in which mentally ill people were confined at that time. Barbed wire covered the transoms of the school. In 1891 three boys fled after being whipped by the schoolmaster and subsequently froze to death in a sudden blizzard. The following year the students were sent home after an outbreak of measles at the school, thus spreading the disease throughout the reservation. Never having developed immunity to diseases that originated in Europe, Indian populations were frequently decimated by outbreaks of such highly contagious illnesses as measles and smallpox. It was estimated that 220 children alone died in this particular epidemic.

In the late 1870s the government implemented another means of enforcing its civilization policies: Indian police. Composed exclusively of reservation Indians, the Indian police were established on many reservations throughout the United States to keep Indians on their reservations, to keep outsiders off, and to see to it that the government's assimilation programs were followed. By the 1890s the Indian police force on the Kiowa-Comanche reservation numbered about 30 men. Among their duties were guarding the school, protecting the agency, and watching for thieves and wandering cattle. In addition, the Indian police were to report to the agent any Kiowa who showed resistance to the government's policies. The force quickly developed into a group dependent upon the federal bureaucracy. Its members had steady jobs on the reservation, where there were very few employment opportunities; moreover, they received extra provisions. When the government wanted the Indians to comply with a new policy, the Indian police were used to enforce the measure.

Despite the government's efforts to destroy their culture, the Kiowa still sought to renew their lives and nation every year with a Sun Dance. By the 1880s, it was becoming more and more difficult to obtain the buffalo necessary for the dance: It was canceled in 1882, and again in 1884 and 1886, because Indian hunters could not find a buffalo. During the summer of 1887 the Kiowa held their last Sun Dance. Known as the *Kodolia Pa Kado*, or Oak Creek Sun Dance, it was made possible only because Charles Goodnight, a Texas rancher who leased reservation lands, supplied the buffalo for $50.

The following year a new agent, E. E. White, banned the Sun Dance in an effort to suppress the Indians' traditional religious practices. When the Kiowa tried to hold the dance again in 1890, Agent Charles E. Adams used the Indian police to prevent the celebration.

The disappearance of the buffalo was perhaps the most difficult change for the Kiowa to comprehend or accept. Many people fervently believed that if they could bring back the buffalo the old way of life would return. In 1882 the former warrior Datekan built a spe-

cial medicine tipi to help the buffalo return. Five years later, Paingya predicted the return of the buffalo and professed his ability to raise people from the dead. When he could not make his own son come back to life or make the buffalo reappear, however, he lost much of the following he had gained.

Despite their dashed hopes, the Kiowa continued to search for explanations of their fate. In early 1890 many embraced the teachings of Wovoka, a medicine man of the Paiute tribe of Nevada. Once when he had been near death, Wovoka claimed, he spoke with the Great Spirit, who told him that the buffalo would return and the whites would disappear if the people performed special rituals that included dancing in a circle for days on end. The

Paingya, an early leader of what was to become the Ghost Dance movement. He displays a hide painting of his 1893 vision promising the buffalo's return.

rituals described by Wovoka became known as the Ghost Dance because they were believed to bring back the dead and bring back the buffalo.

The Kiowa and other Indians of the southern Plains learned of Wovoka's powerful message through an Arapaho, Sitting Bull, who had personally visited the revered medicine man. Encouraged by Sitting Bull's report, the Kiowa sent A'piatan, a nephew of the great chief Lone Wolf, to determine if the Ghost Dance was valid. A'piatan's only child had died recently, and he was eager to see her again. He traveled first to the Sioux, who had embraced the new religion wholeheartedly, and then went on to Nevada to visit the Paiute medicine man himself. Wovoka told the Kiowa warrior that he would not be able to see his daughter: The dance as practiced by Sitting Bull and the Sioux had been altered and was no longer effective. This was in part true: Sioux leaders, facing their own extreme deprivations, had extended Wovoka's concept to include the idea that Indians could become invulnerable to white firearms by wearing special Ghost Dance shirts. Disheartened, A'piatan began the journey home to deliver the sad news to his people.

While A'piatan was away, however, the Kiowa had already begun to follow

Kiowa Ghost Dance, a 1968 watercolor by Stephen Mopope. The tribe ceased practicing the dance after Kiowa A'piatan brought news that Wovoka, the originator of the dance, had now denounced it because changes had made it ineffective.

the teachings of Wovoka as interpreted by Sitting Bull. A dramatic confrontation ensued. Agent Adams wanted to squelch the Kiowa's observance of the Ghost Dance, which government officials considered to be a dangerous rebellion in the guise of a new religion, and he arranged for both A'piatan and Sitting Bull to speak at a council meeting. Here A'piatan repeated what Wovoka had told him and urged the Kiowa to refrain from dancing. Sitting Bull continued to advocate the Ghost Dance, citing as evidence of its effectiveness those who fell into trances while taking part. Because many Indians associated trances and visions with supernatural powers, this was a strong argument in favor of the new ritual. Upon hearing A'piatan's revelations, however, most of the Kiowa sided with their fellow tribesman, and against Sitting Bull, the outsider. They stopped dancing. For his part in the testimony, A'piatan was given a medal by President Benjamin Harrison.

Still another force emerged to threaten Kiowa culture—the General Allotment Act of 1887. Under this law the reservation lands were to be divided into separate units and be distributed, or allotted, to individual Indians. They were to live on and farm their allotments. When each person in the tribe had received a plot, any remaining reservation land was to be sold. The money from the sale of this land would be held in trust for the Indians.

From the beginning the Kiowa, like many other reservation Indians

A'piatan received a medal from President Benjamin Harrison for his role in terminating the Ghost Dance movement.

throughout the country, strongly opposed allotment. The tribe's acting chief, Lone Wolf (a nephew of the former war chief Lone Wolf), informed officials in Washington that his people would go to war if allotment were forced on them. Nevertheless, pressure from non-Indian settlers who wanted to own the land was too strong, and in 1889 Congress authorized a three-member commission to negotiate the allotment of 20 Indian reservations in Oklahoma, including that of the Kiowa. The delegation, known as the Jerome Commission after its chairman, David Jerome, arrived at Fort Sill in September 1892. Among the interpreters employed by the group was Joshua Givens, the son of the Kiowa chief Setangya. Givens had been among the first students

Kiowa students at the Carlisle Indian School in Pennsylvania. Students were forced to wear non-Indian clothing as part of the school's efforts to assimilate them into the mainstream culture.

to attend the Carlisle Indian School, a boarding school for Indian children in Carlisle, Pennsylvania.

Most Kiowa still opposed any form of allotment. Komalty, a Kiowa warrior, argued that 160 acres—the size of the plot each head of a household would receive under the General Allotment Act—was not large enough to allow a Kiowa family to survive, whether by farming or by raising cattle and horses. The 1867 Treaty of Medicine Lodge Creek had guaranteed to each head of a household 320 acres if the Kiowa-Comanche Reservation was ever dis-

solved. Moreover, the treaty had stipulated that three-fourths of the adult men of the tribe had to approve the sale of any land. The Kiowa leader Tohausan told Jerome and the other commissioners that most Kiowa would not sign a document approving the allotment of their reservation.

Nevertheless, the commission got a number of signatures at Fort Sill, including that of Chief Lone Wolf. When it moved on to Anadarko, where most Kiowa lived, opposition was much stronger. A'piatan, the leader of the opposition, accused the commissioners and all those attached to the proceedings of fraud. The Jerome Commission persisted, however, and received 456 signatures out of 562 males considered to be eligible. The official tribal roll, though, showed 725 adult Kiowa and Comanche men.

Soon after the Jerome Commission concluded its work, Joshua Givens, the Indian interpreter, died of unexplained internal bleeding. It was said by some to have been caused by a curse placed on him by a Kiowa medicine man.

It was eight years before the Jerome Agreement was ratified by Congress. In the meantime thousands of land-hungry whites, unable or unwilling to wait for the legal opening of the reservation, began trespassing on the Kiowa's land. They looted the reservation of timber, minerals, and stone and set up farmsteads there. When the Rock Island Railroad put a line through the northern portion of the reservation, small towns sprang up along the route.

In March 1900 the House of Representatives approved a modified version of the Jerome Agreement. This version did not specify the amount of money the Kiowa were to receive for the sale of their unallotted acreage. After the Senate passed its version, a compromise bill was produced and passed by both houses of Congress. This final version guaranteed the combined Kiowa, Kiowa-Apache, and Comanche tribes a minimum of $500,000 for their unallotted land. Among the Kiowa, A'piatan now accepted the agreement, but Lone Wolf did not.

The next year Lone Wolf hired Washington, D.C., attorney William Springer to contest the Jerome Agreement on behalf of the tribe. Springer, who had previously been a member of Congress and a federal judge in Indian Territory, sought an injunction against Secretary of the Interior Ethan Hitchcock to prevent allotment of the Kiowa-Comanche Reservation. But the federal courts ruled against Springer and Lone Wolf, and the U.S. government moved forward with the allotment. Lone Wolf, however, would not give up the fight and appealed the decision. Eventually his case, known as *Lone Wolf v. Hitchcock*, went to the U.S. Supreme Court.

In 1903 the Supreme Court ruled in favor of the U.S. government. Its decision was seen by many as a bold new legal precedent for denying Indian rights. The justices held that Congress had ultimate power over all Indian nations; that powers reserved to the Indians by such agreements as the

Delos K. Lone Wolf, a nephew of Chief Lone Wolf, fought unsuccessfully in court against the Jerome Agreement.

Medicine Lodge treaty could be eliminated by Congress at any time; and that the motives of Congress could not be examined by the court because the so-called Indian problem was a political issue, not a legal one.

By 1906 the Kiowa-Comanche Reservation had been allotted. The heads of Kiowa households had received 160-acre plots, and the 480,000 acres of unallotted lands had been sold for more than $4 million. This money was to be managed for the Indians by the federal government.

For the most part, the Kiowa were now on their own: There were no more government rations to be distributed. But even though the land, like the buffalo, had been taken away from them, the Kiowa Nation remained to face the 20th century. ▲

Father Isidore Ricklin, founder of St. Patrick's Mission, in Council with Chiefs, *a mural painted in 1929 by Kiowa Six artist Jack Hokeah.*

COMING OUT
AGAIN

Direct Examination by Mr. Miskovsky: Now I will ask you to again examine the signature opposite 318 and state to the Indian Claims Commission whether or not that is your handwriting. Is that your handwriting?

Yellow Boy Tonemah: No, I do not write my name like that.

So the testimony went before the Indian Claims Commission (ICC), a special tribunal created by Congress in 1946 to investigate and settle claims by American Indians of previous injustices perpetrated on them in order to take their lands. Cases brought before the ICC generally dealt with breaches of the treaties or agreements between the U.S. government and one or more groups of Indians. The Kiowa were among the first Indian nations to press their claims. Of particular concern to them were violations of several treaties and the fraud perpetrated by the Jerome Agreement. They saw a chance to right the wrong done them by the Supreme Court's 1903 decision in *Lone Wolf v. Hitchcock*, and

in bringing this challenge they continued to show their cultural tenacity.

Although the 20th century was a time of suffering for the Kiowa, it was also the beginning of a cultural renewal. It was a time of coming out again.

Before the renewal, however, came the suffering. From 1906, the year when the reservation was allotted, to 1936, when allotment was halted for the Kiowa, the Kiowa homelands were under attack. Before allotment, individual Kiowas held a total of 2,968,893 acres of land in southeastern Oklahoma, and another 553,680 acres of pasture were owned by the tribes. By 1936, when allotment was completed and restrictions were placed on the sale of Indian-held land, the Kiowa Nation had shriveled to 1,022,991 acres plus 33,431 acres of common pasturage. More than 65 percent of individual Kiowa holdings had been lost to non-Indians, and 93 percent of their pasturage was gone.

The Kiowa economy disintegrated. The people had never been keen on farming, but some had taken to raising cattle, only to be forced out by the droughts of the early and late 1920s. Although epidemics were much less frequent and starvation was not as serious a threat as it had been previously, the Kiowa, bereft of much of their land, became mired in rural poverty.

Not even the discovery of oil and gas on their lands brought prosperity. They made their first leases of mining rights in 1914 and took in an average of $200,000 per year. But the fees were small compared to the profits reaped by the companies that extracted the oil and gas from the Indians' lands and sold them at very high prices. Moreover, the lease revenues were managed by the federal government. Few benefits were realized by the majority of Kiowa, however, because most of the funds were retained by the government to administer the Kiowa-Comanche agency.

The Kiowa's leaders were unable to ameliorate their social and economic problems. In fact, Kiowa political institutions were adrift. Without war honors, without the hunt, and without an identifiable means of sustaining an economy, there was no longer a basis

Drilling an oil well in Lawton, Oklahoma, 1901. The Kiowa realized few benefits from the discovery of oil on their land because much of the resulting income was kept by the government for administrative expenses.

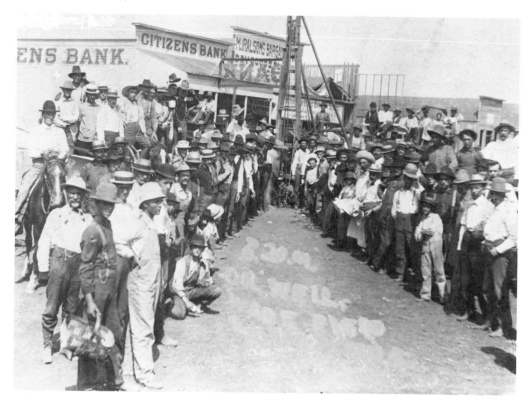

for political power. The traditional system of ranked societies that had for centuries given structure to Kiowa life now had little meaning. The members of the Koitsenko society could no longer be chosen. The reservation was gone. Only the agency remained, and it was through the Kiowa-Comanche-Apache agent that leadership was chosen over the next 30 years. The agent chose representatives from each tribe to constitute the Kiowa-Comanche-Apache Inter-tribal Business Committee. Five Kiowas, two Kiowa-Apaches, and six Comanches composed the committee. Although prominent men held these positions, they did not necessarily embody Kiowa, Kiowa-Apache, or Comanche opinion. Their position was a difficult one: They lacked the sanction of their own people, and in addition they had no power to overrule the agent. Without real authority, there was no possibility of leadership.

The Kiowa had little political or diplomatic use for the Business Committee. They recognized that it was merely a semiofficial channel for carrying out policies formulated by the Bureau of Indian Affairs. When important issues arose, individual Kiowa tried to influence local Oklahoma officials, but that was difficult because at that time Indians were excluded by state laws from voting in Oklahoma elections. Until 1936, using individual influence was the only political option available to them.

In view of the economic disasters and political powerlessness experi-

Three Kiowa who chose not to follow traditional beliefs: Lucius Ben Aitsan (left) became a missionary and established the Saddle Mountain Baptist Church, where Odlepauh (seated), eldest son of Principal Chief Satanta, served as a deacon. San-co (right) was an early Kiowa convert to Christianity.

enced by the Kiowa in the first decades of the 20th century, it is not surprising that they turned inward to find comfort and security. Self-examination led to two significant developments in Kiowa life, one religious and the other cultural: the spread of the Native American Church and the stirrings of modern cultural revival and adaptation.

For several years missionaries had attempted to convert the Kiowa to various branches of Christianity. First to arrive were the Episcopalians, who settled in the southern part of the reservation around 1880 and had some success in winning converts. Baptists and Methodists, who came somewhat later, also found converts. They built missions and schools in Kiowa country, and Kiowa became church members and even ministers. Lucius Aitsan, the son of a Mexican captive named Mokeen and one of Satanta's former wives, was the first Kiowa Baptist minister. Similarly, Albert Horse, born in a tipi in the Wichita Mountains, was converted to Methodism after he was sent to the Methodist school at Anadarko. In 1930 he became a minister at the Mt. Scott Kiowa Methodist Church, which had been founded by a number of Kiowa, including Luther Sahmount and his wife Virginia Stumbling Bear.

But for most Kiowa, mainstream Christianity was not a satisfactory answer to the stresses of the early 20th century. Instead they turned to worship in the Native American Church, which centers on the use of peyote, a cactus native to Mexico and Texas. Ingestion of peyote buttons causes purging and, for some worshipers, hallucinogenic visions. It has been used as a religious sacrament among Indians in Mexico for centuries, and in the late 19th century peyote rituals began to spread among Indians north of the border. Even though the Kiowa used fewer Christian rites in their services than did many other Indians, the ceremony nonetheless combined Christian with tradi-

tional Indian religious practices. In the peyote observances, the Kiowa were able to attain a feeling of personal significance because each individual could freely pursue his or her own special visions. This gave the Kiowa the possibility of saving their cultural traditions within an organized religious framework.

In many ways peyotism helped bind various Indian groups together, giving them a sense of unity. This pan-Indian religious movement was not unlike the Ghost Dance of the 19th century in its rapid spread among Indians of different backgrounds. At first both Oklahoma authorities and members of Congress tried to suppress the ceremonies. They did not understand the role played by peyote in a religious context. In 1918 peyotists from the Kiowa, Oto, and Arapaho tribes met in Cheyenne, Oklahoma, to discuss the threats facing their religious observances. They decided to incorporate the Native American Church in order to save and defend Kiowa and other Indian religious and cultural traditions. Incorporation legally registered their religion and thus eventually brought their practices under the protection of the First Amendment of the U.S. Constitution. Over the years, numerous cases in a number of states have affirmed this protection in rulings that deny states the right to prohibit religious use of peyote.

Among the first trustees of the Native American Church were Kiowa Charley and Delos Lone Wolf. Trustees were part of the organizational struc-

(continued on page 89)

PAINTERS OF THE PLAINS

For centuries the Kiowa have been artists. On the plains, they used crushed colored earths and rocks as paint. Women painted geometric designs on containers made of rawhide (parfleche), and men painted the buffalo-hide coverings of their tipis to illustrate battle scenes, visions, and their history. The tipi designs belonged to prominent men—chiefs, leading warriors, medicine men—and were passed down from father to son. The design might represent a family's "medicine," or protection against bad fortune. After the buffalo were nearly exterminated, tipi covers were made of canvas but painted in the same way.

A few Kiowa chiefs painted designs onto buffalo hide to represent important events of half-year periods; later, such calendars were drawn with colored pencil on paper. In the 1870s, after a number of Kiowa warriors were imprisoned at Fort Marion, Florida, they learned to draw and paint with new materials. From 1891 to 1904, James Mooney, an ethnologist with the Smithsonian Institution, had some Kiowa men paint their family designs on model tipis made of buckskin. This project helped to preserve Kiowa tipi painting for all time.

In the 1920s, five young Kiowas were encouraged to study at the University of Oklahoma School of Art. The Kiowa Five were Jack Hokeah, Spencer Asah, James Auchiah, Stephen Mopope, and Monroe Tsatoke. They inspired a number of associates, including Lois (Bou-ge-tah) Smokey, sometimes considered a "Kiowa Sixth."

Kiowa today continue to be artists, illustrating the symbols of their history with modern materials.

A headdress or bonnet case of rawhide, painted with a geometric design.

Drawing of the Sun Dance, made in a notebook by a Kiowa warrior named Wo-haw, who was imprisoned at Fort Marion in the 1870s.

The buffalo-hide calendar drawn by Anko around 1864 to 1893. In the 1890s, Anko recreated his calendar in pencil on brown paper at the request of ethnologist James Mooney.

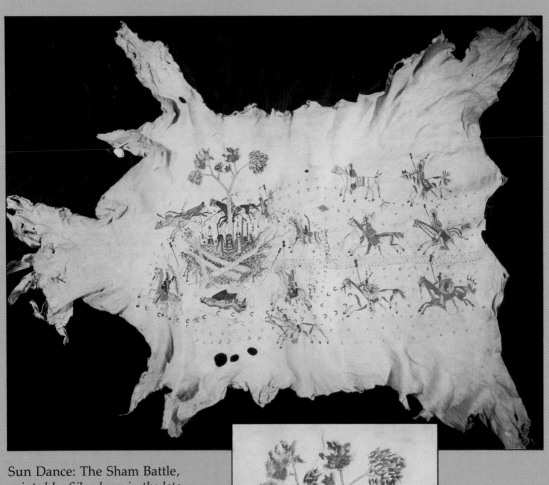

Sun Dance: The Sham Battle,
painted by Silverhorn in the late
19th century. Silverhorn was a
leader of the Sun Dance ritual as
well as an artist; he was also the un-
cle and first art teacher of Kiowa
Five painter Stephen Mopope.

Detail from Sun Dance.   83

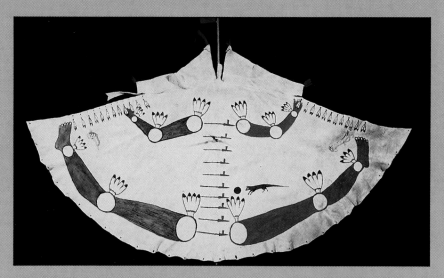

The unusual Leg-Picture Tipi captures a vision seen by Fair-Haired Old Man. The disembodied legs and arms are adorned by feathers.

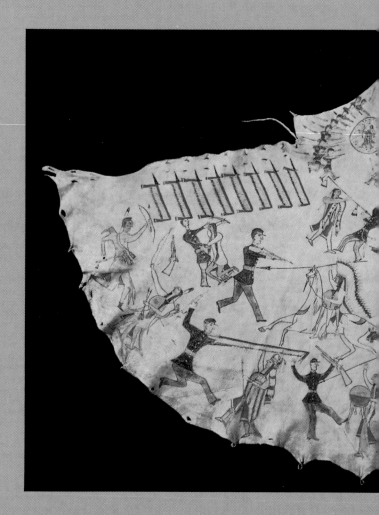

Underwater-Monster Tipi. According to Kiowa legend, the horned fish, or Zemoguani, might lurk in caverns to kill a swimmer.

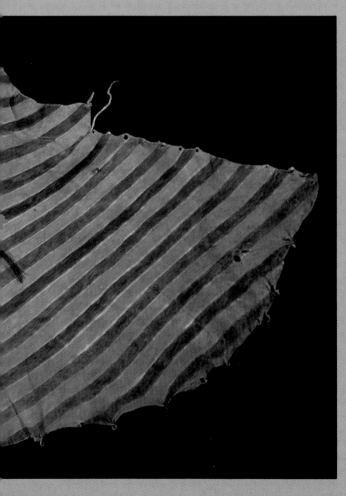

The Battle-Picture Tipi of Little Bluff, the Kiowa principal chief who died in 1866. The painting records courageous acts by several Kiowa against enemy warriors and U.S. soldiers.

The Kiowa Five painted scenes of their people's history and experience. Asah, Hokeah, and Mopope were dancers; Aukiah and Tsatoke were singers and drummers. They were concerned with perpetuating Kiowa traditions in all of the arts.

Stephen Mopope's Indian Dancer.

Jack Hokeah's Chasing Evil Spirits.

Lois (Bou-ge-tah) Smokey's Kiowa Family.

Monroe Tsatoke's Dance of the Dog Soldiers.

Tribal Memories, *by Robert Red-bird (born 1939), incorporates the fan of the peyote ritual with dream-like images of the buffalo and eagle. A new generation continues the Kiowa's artistic traditions.*

Sharron Ahtone Harjo's Re-turn Them Safely to Home, *a 1971 work in acrylic on canvas, commemorates a historic event of the 1860s, in which Kiowa warriors captured a prized possession—a beaded lance—of an enemy tribe.*

(continued from page 80)

ture required by incorporation. Most of the trustees were Indians who had been educated at Carlisle Indian School in Pennsylvania and who were devoted to learning about and preserving traditional Indian ways.

The Native American Church is a basically Christian religious organization that is still active among the Kiowa today. From its start, it provided the Kiowa with a means of transition. Kiowa were always aware of the conflict between their traditions and the outside world, and their success in maintaining the inner strength needed to resist the cultural onslaught was truly remarkable. Through the peyote ceremony, self-doubt could be both expressed and contained. One prayer reveals the personal crisis faced by all Kiowa at the turn of the century, when their peyote ceremony began to flourish:

Let us see, is this real,
This life I am living, is it real?
You, Sayn-daw-kee, who dwells
    everywhere,
Let us see, is this real, this life I am
    living?

The ability of the Native American Church to help the Kiowa deal with cultural conflicts was exemplified by the life of Paul Zotom or Podala dalte (Biter). When Zotom was young he had been a Kiowa warrior. Captured in 1875, he was sent to Fort Marion, Florida, where he became a bugler, dancer, and artist. In 1878 he was sent to Hampton National and Agricultural Institute,

Late 19th-century Kiowa artist Paul Zotom, who spent much of his life attempting to harmonize Indian and non-Indian ways of life, making a model tipi.

a school for blacks in Virginia that had recently started an Indian department. From there he went on to a Christian private school, Paris Hill, in New York where he became an Episcopalian. In 1881 he was sent back home to the Kiowa to head a mission. After a while, he began to wear traditional Kiowa clothes and participated in a Sun Dance. Outraged, the Episcopalian authorities removed Zotom from his positions at the mission. Zotom then simultaneously joined the Baptists and the Native American Church. He made his living primarily as an artist and exhibited his painted shields and tipis at an exposition showcasing Indian cul-

(continued on page 92)

PEYOTE RELIGION AND
THE NATIVE AMERICAN CHURCH

Prominent in the religious observances of the Kiowa is the ritual use of *peyote* (pay-OH-tee), a part of the mescal cactus, a plant native to the southwestern U.S. and Mexico. This spineless cactus produces small outgrowths called buttons; these are dried, then chewed and swallowed in ceremonies that are part of what is sometimes called "the peyote religion" or Peyotism. The buttons contain substances with hallucinogenic properties, so that ingesting them may cause visions. Traditionally, Indians in much of North America, and especially those of the Plains, believed that visions were a sign of supernatural power.

Peyotism originated among the Indians of Mexico and spread northward through social contact between tribes. Sometime around the 1860s, the Mescalero Apache of southern Texas introduced the peyote ritual to their allies, the Comanche, and within a decade it passed from the Comanche to the Kiowa. The ceremony continued to spread to other Plains tribes, and eventually Peyotism became (and remains) the largest intertribal Indian religion in North America.

The Kiowa practice the Little Moon peyote ceremony. Preparations for the ceremony take place during the day, and the ceremony itself begins at sundown and lasts until after sunrise on the following day.

A special tipi is set up, and within it the participants build an earthen altar in the shape of a crescent moon, and a sitting area lined with sprigs of blue-green sagebrush. A fire burns before the altar, and on the altar itself is placed the cactus, which is referred to as "Father Peyote." At least three officials preside over the ceremony: the road chief, the drum chief, and the fireman.

The road chief is the ritual leader. He begins and ends the ceremony with songs (each of which is sung four times), calls for water at midnight and sunrise, and also calls for the morning breakfast that ends the ceremony. As part of his office, he carries ritual instruments including a staff, an eagle-tail fan, a gourd rattle, and a sack containing the peyote buttons. The drum chief carries drumsticks and a water-filled drum and accompanies the road chief and the male participants as each takes turns in singing. During this singing, the peyote buttons are eaten.

The fireman carries an eagle feather fan. At midnight he brings in water, which the participants drink after praying over it for tribal success and health. After this, the road chief steps outside the tipi, blows upon an eagle-bone whistle, and prays to the four corners of the earth. He returns to the tipi and the singing resumes, continuing until sunrise. At this time, water is brought in by a woman, who is ceremonially honored; according to myth, it was a woman who first introduced peyote to her tribe.

A woman also brings in breakfast, over which prayers are again offered. The ceremony ends when water is poured from the drum onto the fire, and the road chief sings a prescribed quitting song. The tipi may also be disassembled and then moved, to signify that it is no longer a place of worship.

As the ritual has developed since the 1800s, it has absorbed some aspects of Christianity. For example, the crucifix is incorporated in the cross-bar of the road chief's staff. The ritual use of peyote has sometimes caused conflict

Tipi in which the peyote ritual was conducted. This tipi was opened up so that ethnologist James Mooney could photograph it in 1892.

Detail from a Kiowa hide painting showing the position of peyote-ritual participants around the crescent-shaped altar.

with non-Indian officials, who have at times considered peyote a contraband drug and, on occasion, prosecuted participants. However, the use of peyote is part of an established belief system of numerous tribes, with a shared set of symbols and ritual instruments. Its use in religious ceremonies is fully protected by the freedom of religion provision of the U.S. Constitution. The Native American Church, which practices Peyotism, has been legally recognized in Oklahoma, the Kiowa's home state, since 1918.

(continued from page 89)

ture held in Omaha in 1898. Zotom died in 1913. He had lived his entire life in transition.

Zotom's commitment to Kiowa culture in his art was a form of cultural preservation that other Kiowa would later follow. In 1928 Monroe Tsatoke, Stephen Mopope, Spencer Asah, James Auchiah, Jack Hokeah, and Bou-ge-tah Smokey entered the art school at the University of Oklahoma. Encouraged by a federal government field matron assigned to the Kiowa, these young artists recorded the War Dance, the Dance of the Dog Soldiers, the Peyote Ceremony, and other rituals and legends. Known as the Kiowa Six, they founded a modern school of Indian painting, setting an example not only for subsequent Kiowa painters but for artists in other media and from other tribes across the country.

Early on, the artistic revival of the Kiowa Six combined with other efforts to renew the old ways. In the 1930s the Gourd Dancers' clan, which had once been in charge of the various dances performed in the ceremony of the Sun Dance, was revived. The clan had stopped its activities after the Sun Dance was prohibited, but it now rehearsed and performed in public, even though the Sun Dance could no longer be held. In 1931 the first American Indian Exposition was held at Anadarko. Dancing, crafts exhibits and demonstrations, archery contests, horse races, and pageants were organized into a celebration of the Indian culture. This was an especially important event for Oklahoma Indians—it marked the first time they were confident that their cultural heritage could be publicly shown. Traditions that might have been forgotten could now be protected and revived. The Kiowa played an important part in this event; despite difficult times, they were held together by their attempts to save their traditional culture.

In the early 1930s a change came to the federal government. Franklin D. Roosevelt's administration brought a "New Deal" to a nation wracked by the unemployment and distress of the Great Depression. Within Roosevelt's administration were some non-Indians who recognized that Indians needed to have a restored political function and a means of developing their own economy. The decades-old concept of cultural repression was being reexamined. A leader of those new ideas was John Collier, who became Roosevelt's commissioner of Indian affairs. Collier proposed an Indian New Deal and legislation known as the Wheeler-Howard Act or Indian Reorganization Act (IRA) came before the Congress. The proposed IRA would put a halt to the allotment of Indian lands, allow new lands to be purchased for tribal ownership by Indians, create a fund to be used by Indians for agricultural and industrial development in their communities, and offer Indians expanded educational opportunities. At the same time, a mechanism for establishing elected tribal governments was to be set up, and legal protection would be extended to the expression of Indian cul-

The Kiowa Six artists, with followers, in their dance regalia. Front row, left to right: *Monroe Tsatoke, Jack Hokeah, and Susie Peters.* Second row: *Dr. Oscar Jacobson, Bou-ge-tah Smokey, Spencer Asah, James Auchiah, and Stephen Mopope.*

tures and religions. John Collier, with the members of the Commission on Indian Affairs, set out across the country to explain the IRA to Indians.

On March 20, 1934, Collier and the commission met with Indians in Anadarko to discuss the proposed Wheeler-Howard Act. Because the Kiowa had chosen to live in the most rural parts of their reservation lands and had not congregated in cities, they were more isolated than most other Oklahoma Indians and had retained more tribal cohesion. The Bureau of Indian Affairs normally kept a close watch on property belonging to wealthy Indians, but the Kiowa had very few large property owners. As a result, their contact with BIA officials had been limited. Consequently, the federal government had little influence over them, and some Kiowas actively opposed the Wheeler-

Howard Act and its extension to Oklahoma Indians.

Opposition was led by Jasper Saunkeah and Delos Lone Wolf. At the last congress called to discuss the Wheeler-Howard Act at Anadarko, Delos Lone Wolf argued that such legislation would set the Kiowa back another 60 years. He said he would "rather pay taxes and be a man among men than a useless Indian forever." He and others opposed reestablishment of a reservation and consolidation of property for the benefit of the entire Kiowa nation. Delos Lone Wolf, a graduate of Carlisle Indian School, a trustee of the peyote-celebrating Native American Church, a football player on the all-Indian team founded by Olympic athlete Jim Thorpe, and a successful farmer, had made the transition. He had adapted to the new rules, and he was suspicious of any attempt at change.

Despite Kiowa opposition, Congress passed the Indian Reorganization Act in 1934, and in 1936 it was extended to Oklahoma Native Americans under what came to be called the Oklahoma Indian Welfare Act. Allotment ceased and the massive loss of Kiowa lands ended. Some lands that had been taken earlier but were not being used were restored. Tribal governments were established. For the Kiowa this meant that the Inter-tribal Business Committee could become for the first time an expression of tribal opinion. Their representatives on the committee were now to be elected by the individual tribes rather than appointed by a fed-

eral agent. From this experiment in representative democracy evolved individual tribal governments for the Kiowa and Comanche.

The new laws also provided for ways to revitalize Indian economies and to protect Indian ethnic identities. A revolving credit fund was established to allow Indians to borrow money from the federal government in order to set up small businesses. Individual Kiowa got Kiowa approval for business ven-

John Collier (far right), commissioner of Indian affairs under Franklin D. Roosevelt, attends a 1939 session in which Kiowa musicians made recordings of traditional music for the BIA archives.

tures through the Inter-tribal Business Committee. As loans depleted the fund, it was replenished by federal funds, and its stability was backed by federal guarantees. The Inter-tribal Business Committee suddenly found itself with the authority to borrow money from a $10 million fund, to set up loan committees made up of Indian members, and to plan new forms of economic development. The IRA also protected Indian religions and encouraged artistic expression.

The Kiowa benefited directly from the Oklahoma Indian Welfare Act. A tribal government evolved that, although not based upon tradition, encouraged the development of political leadership. Economic hope came to the tribe. A rural economic development plan began to function. Young Kiowa could pursue education without having to sacrifice their Kiowa traditions. But the reforms of the New Deal did not produce overnight improvements. The Great Depression continued to affect the economy of the entire nation through the 1930s, and a drought that turned much of the nation's midsection, including Oklahoma, into a dust bowl restricted all that might have been accomplished. It was not until after World War II that a fully functioning Indian New Deal was firmly in place.

By 1950 the Kiowa were emerging again. They were divided into social and economic classes that had some resemblance to the different classes of their traditional society, and the old names for these classes were used again. An upper class, the onde, included Kiowa who had held on to land, gained some wealth, and received war honors either during World War I or World War II. Lower classes included two groups: the kaan, who had no wealth but shared the values of the onde and who may have participated in war; and the dapone, those without wealth or social status. In the post–World War II years, social mobility could occur, but it was a slow process. Wealth tended to stay in very few hands among the Kiowa, but young onde sought opportunities for economic and political advancement.

Revival also occurred within Kiowa culture. The societies, abandoned for more than half a century, were organized once again. The Black Leggings Society, a warriors' group that had ceased to function after the Kiowa ended their war activities on the Plains, began to meet once more. The new Black Leggings Society consisted of veterans of the First and Second World Wars. The Kiowa tribal government formally recognized the Gourd Dance Society, which had survived unofficially since the 1930s. Now it was opened to more Kiowa than it had been previously. It celebrated its annual gathering at the time of year when a Sun Dance would in earlier days have brought the Kiowa together. The new ceremony, held in Carnegie, began when a lance was thrust into the ground and the dancers pledged to give meat to the assembled camps, rituals that echoed those of the past. Now, too, many more Kiowa became involved with the American Indian Exposition, a pan-Indian fair held each summer in Anadarko.

Perhaps the best example of Kiowa acculturation can be seen in the Kiowa language. Automobiles became commonplace in rural Kiowa country after the war, and they came to be known as *awdlemodlbidl*. In Kiowa, three words or expressions came together to form the word for automobile: *gyesadl*, meaning "it is hot," *hodl*, meaning "to kill," and *k'awndedl*, meaning "badly." The "bad, hot killing machine" transformed Kiowa country along with the rest of

rural America, and the Kiowa recognized the car in their own language for what it was.

Equally strong and forceful was the tradition of the 10 medicine bundles. These had been kept sacred even during the darkest hours of cultural repression. In the 1930s one of the bundles was destroyed by fire. Some of the elder Kiowa believe that World War II was due in part to this calamity. Each bundle has two keepers, a man and a woman. These positions are inherited. The bundles symbolize cultural continuity with the past, and the keepers are

Led by a uniformed, flag-bearing serviceman, Kiowa women participate in a War Mothers' Victory Dance during World War II, a ceremony that united traditional ritual with contemporary patriotism.

respected members of the Kiowa Nation. In the 1950s most of the bundles were kept by peyotist families who were trying to maintain Kiowa ways within a modern world.

By then the Kiowa had choices. Gone were the days of the siege. They no longer had to worry about total loss of their lands, starvation, or cultural suppression. Kiowa were able to find employment off the reservation. Young people could join the army or attend a school for advanced occupational training. The Kiowa had more religious freedom, and their tribal government provided some degree of political expression. Nevertheless, these opportunities often caused disputes within Kiowa political institutions.

The political divisions within the Kiowa surfaced openly in the 1950s, but their roots went deep into the past and the divisions continue to the present day. Two general groups emerged: progressives and conservatives. Progressives are predominantly Christian Kiowa, frequently young onde, who live in the southern part of Kiowa country near Lawton. Some peyotists are progressives, but within this faction they are a minority. Many progressives are employed by government agencies. When in power, progressives attempt to maintain control through the distribution of wealth. They are not the keepers of any medicine bundles or of the most sacred object, the tai-me. Sometimes called the "peacefuls," the progressives serve as contacts with the non-Indian world. They stress education and accommodation, working with and serving the white community.

Among the progressives are some descendants of Kicking Bird, a prominent war chief. In the 1870s Kicking Bird and Sitting Bear were political rivals. A Quaker missionary, Thomas Battey, came to the reservation and attempted first to convert Sitting Bear and his band. But he insulted Sitting Bear and was told to leave. Kicking Bird then invited Battey to live with his band on Medicine Creek near Fort Sill. Kicking Bird was converted to Christianity, and his band's descendants became Methodists and Baptists in the Mount Scott area. This group provided the basis of progressive Kiowa politics. The feud between the relatives of Kicking Bird and those of Sitting Bear still continues.

Sitting Bear's followers and relatives constitute a significant number of the conservatives. Concentrated in three areas near the Washita River (Carnegie, Fort Cobb, and Mountain View), the conservatives are a close-knit group. They were opposed to allotment and receptive to the Native American Church. Although allotment was abolished as a federal government policy in the 1930s, Kiowa continue to remember the great suffering it caused, and it remains an issue in Kiowa politics. Keepers of the tai-me and the medicine bundles are conservatives. The descendants of A'piatan, Dohasan, and Delos Lone Wolf are prominent conservatives in Carnegie. When they are in power, they maintain their influence by distributing favors. The kaan, those who have little property, are often recipients of such favors and thus constitute an important base of conservative support. The conservatives have generally held power over the progressives because they represent to many Kiowa a valid effort to defend the cultural values of the past. Meanwhile, the conservatives have encouraged progressives to develop contacts with whites, which makes it possible for the conservatives to remain an unknown element to the white community. Conservatives have controlled the Inter-tribal Business Committee, the loan committee, and the directorship of the Anadarko Indian Exposition. The Kiowa tribal chairman has most often been a conservative.

Two federal policies challenged the political leadership of the Kiowa from the 1950s through the 1970s. The first was "termination." During the administration of President Dwight D. Eisenhower, the policies instituted by the Wheeler-Howard Act were halted as the federal government attempted to put an end to all programs benefiting Indians. Under this new policy, ostensibly intended to provide greater freedom for individual Indians, selected tribes lost federal recognition and thus were effectively terminated, losing eligibility for federal programs. The second policy was relocation. The federal government offered incentives, such as free one-way transportation, cash gifts, or promises of jobs, to lure young Indians away from reservations and rural Indian communities to urban areas. The stated goal was for the new urban In-

dian to gain training and skills in order to qualify for jobs that were not available in rural areas.

Both factions of the Kiowa viewed termination as a threat to their nation. Progressives, however, considered termination to be inevitable and believed the Kiowa needed to plan for it. Conservatives were more adamant in their opposition. They believed that the use of delaying tactics would eventually prove effective, and this indeed is what happened: By refusing to cooperate with the federal government, the Kiowa successfully avoided termination. Government bureaucrats turned their attention to other tribes, with whom they perceived a greater chance for success. Those tribes suffered greatly: They lost all of their land, lost jobs as government agencies and offices closed, saw educational opportunities in their neighborhoods end as federal funding for their schools evaporated, and became dependent upon government welfare payments.

Relocation to a city, however, was a much different matter. While the conservatives resisted the concept, progressives could see its advantages. Progressive Kiowa cooperated with the Bureau of Indian Affairs to encourage young Kiowa to strike out for a better life, provided that they remembered their relatives in rural Oklahoma.

Many Kiowa moved to various nearby cities, such as Oklahoma City and Dallas, but some were encouraged to go as far away as California. A Kiowa who moves to Los Angeles is the subject of the novel *House Made of Dawn*, by N. Scott Momaday, which won the Pulitzer Prize for fiction in 1969. The novel tells the tragic story of how the life of a Kiowa unravels as he attempts to adjust to an urban environment.

Many California-bound Kiowa moved to the San Francisco Bay area. By 1964 at least 150 Kiowa were living in Oakland, San Francisco, and San Jose. Their move had been sponsored by the Employment Assistance Program of the Bureau of Indian Affairs, the federal agency that had been established to deal with all relocation. In the cities, most Kiowa took jobs as carpenters or manual laborers. They worked hard but did not try for further advancement, as security and a decent wage were enough to satisfy them. The average annual wage of a Kiowa family in the San Francisco Bay area during the early 1960s was $7,600, about the same as that of their non-Indian neighbors. Many of these Kiowa owned a modest home.

However, cultural life proved to be a struggle for the Christian off-reservation Kiowa. They did not find satisfaction in churches where the pastor could not speak to them in Kiowa. Although they had previously ignored the peyote ceremonies and large social get-togethers such as powwows, most of the newly urban Kiowa now missed their culture, and they searched for an identity. For many this meant returning to Oklahoma or joining other urban Indians in groups where they could re-create old cultural ideals.

In 1960 the Kiowa faced another dilemma that engendered political disputes, but at least this problem was the result of an episode that had a positive outcome: The Indian Claims Commission finally ruled in favor of the Kiowa's suit for damages resulting from the fraudulent Jerome Agreement. The dilemma was, what were the Kiowa to do with the nearly $2 million awarded to them?

Testimony from the Kiowa had begun in 1949. Litigation proved complex and lengthy. The federal government asserted that any award to the Kiowa should be used to offset the more than $1.5 million charged to them for depredations committed against white settlers. Previous decisions for other tribes had allowed such offsets, but the Kiowa won in spite of numerous delays and the Supreme Court holding against them in *Lone Wolf v. Hitchcock*. The Indian Claims Commission decided in its Kiowa case that depredation offsets were contrary to the purpose of its claims proceedings. This ruling paved the way for claims decisions in favor of other Indian litigants as well.

Now the Kiowa were to get $2 million. Progressives urged placing the money in a trust fund to be held by the federal government so that the money could be invested in projects for the benefit of the Kiowa Nation as a whole. They wanted some of the money used to educate young Kiowa and to plan rural economic development. Conservatives disagreed, arguing instead for immediate distribution of the money on a per capita (per person) basis, because most of the people were poor and needed the funds immediately. The conservatives prevailed. In the spring of 1960, 10,000 Kiowa, Kiowa-Apache, and Comanche received individual checks of nearly $200 each. This amount did not go very far.

The euphoria brought about by both the ICC victory and the victory over termination efforts ended for the Kiowa with the stark economic reality of the 1970s. At the Anadarko agency in 1970, 23 percent of all Indians were unemployed, and fewer than 100 were employed in nongovernment positions. Only about a fifth of the Indian families lived in housing equipped with standard plumbing, electricity, and similar features. Almost half of all Kiowa youths failed to complete high school. Personal income in 1970 averaged $1,139 (compared to the national per capita of $4,808), and almost two-fifths of that came in the form of land-lease revenues, veterans' benefits, or public assistance. It was a bleak picture, but it nevertheless represented a limited improvement over their situation at any point earlier in the century.

Today most Kiowa reside on former reservation lands in seven rural enclaves surrounded by white settlements. The Kiowa population is expanding, but their landholdings remain the same. Most have a grade-school education, and younger Kiowa are encouraged to go to college. Many own cars and can speak English. At the same time, Oklahoma Kiowa maintain

N. Scott Momaday, author of the 1969 Pulitzer Prize–winning novel House Made of Dawn and other works, is a professor of English at the University of Arizona in Tucson.

their cultural identity and their sense of community. The Kiowa language is being taught to young people, and traditional tales and customs are being recorded. Kiowas continue to dance their old dances and to keep alive their social and religious practices.

The largest of the seven Kiowa settlements is Carnegie, whose residents are generally peyotists. Carnegie is also the home of many influential conservatives, and its families are closely re-

Kirke Kickingbird, formerly an attorney in Washington, D.C., and a U.S. representative to the United Nations, has returned to private practice and his Kiowa heritage in Oklahoma.

lated to families in smaller communities at Fort Cobb, Mountain View, and Lone Wolf, which is the least important and most isolated of the Kiowa neighborhoods. The Mount Scott area is primarily Christian and the home of most prominent progressives. It is attached to the smaller Southeast Kiowa County settlement. The seventh settlement, at Anadarko, is isolated in another way. Mostly Christian, its residents include many intermarried Kiowa-white couples and relatives of Carlisle graduates. The people living here generally do not feel close to the people in the other Kiowa communities.

The Kiowa's major problems today continue to be economic. They need jobs—and the training to be able to get and hold those jobs. Better health care

and nutrition would improve the health of the many people who suffer from chronic heart trouble and diabetes. The future of the Kiowa, said tribal chairman Pressly Ware in 1982, depends upon their youth becoming educated and returning to help the Kiowa solve modern problems.

After Ware's term as tribal chairman ended, there was a dispute over the election of his successor. Ace Sahmaunt received the greater number of votes but was denied the post when it was charged that he had outstanding debts to the tribe. His opponent, Glenn Hamilton, was elected to the disputed post in 1987. Ultimately, however, Sahmaunt showed that he had indeed paid his debts, and he was elected tribal chairman in 1988.

Kiowa today are accommodating both the past and the future. This can be seen in the lives of three very different people. Belle Keyitah, a resident of Carnegie, Oklahoma, graduated from the Santa Fe Art Institute in 1938— one of the first Indians to do so. For many years Keyitah served as a counselor at Haskell Institute, an Indian boarding school in Lawrence, Kansas. There she enhanced the art of beadwork and of embroidering the shawls worn by women in traditional Kiowa dances. Now retired, she works at home, where she spends much of her time designing beaded necklaces, medallions, and headbands and teaching the Kiowa language. Belle Keyitah and her art are living remnants of the Kiowa past.

Perry Horse is another Kiowa who went "abroad." Born in a tent outside Carnegie, he attended Haskell Institute and worked for the BIA before spending three years in the army. He trained as a court reporter and served in Korea. After his discharge, he returned to the BIA to work in the agency's education office. While living in Washington, D.C., he studied art at the Corcoran Gallery and decided to become a painter. A descendant of Methodist ministers, he and his Cherokee wife have attended Native American Church services. Although Perry Horse hardly speaks Kiowa at all and continues to live in Washington, he knows he is a modern Kiowa. "I think of myself as a Kiowa first, an American citizen second," he says.

Kirke Kickingbird is a Kiowa of the future. He grew up in Kiowa country, earned a B.A. and law degree from the University of Oklahoma, and passed the Oklahoma bar examination. He has served as general counsel of the American Indian Policy Review Commission, chairman of the Indian Law Committee of the Federal Bar Association, director of the Center for the Development of American Indian Law, and represen-

tative of the United States at the 1977 United Nations Geneva Conference on Discrimination Against Indigenous Populations. After much diplomatic success in Washington, D.C., he has returned to Oklahoma and his Kiowa heritage to practice law.

Thus, the 20th century has seen the Kiowa emerging again. They have survived the worst of times and embraced the best of times. From their first emergence in ancient times to their assumption of the Plains Indian culture, from their era of migrations to the decades of struggle and resistance, the Kiowa have prevailed. Throughout their history, they have kept their culture, spirit, and sense of national identity.

N. Scott Momaday expresses this self-assurance well:

Noon in the intermountain plain:
There is scant telling of the marsh—
A log, hollow and weather-stained,
An insect at the mouth, and moss—
Yet waters rise against the roots,
Stand brimming to the stalks. What
    moves?
What moves on this archaic force
Was wild and welling at the source.

It is the Kiowa. ▲

BIBLIOGRAPHY

Boyd, Maurice. *Kiowa Voices*. Vol. 1, *Ceremonial Dance, Ritual and Song*. Fort Worth: Texas Christian University Press, 1981.

———. *Kiowa Voices*. Vol. 2, *Myths, Legends and Folk Tales*. Fort Worth: Texas Christian University Press, 1983.

Brown, Dee. *Bury My Heart at Wounded Knee*. New York: Washington Square Press, 1981.

Levy, Jerrold E. *After Custer: Kiowa Political and Social Organization from the Reservation to the Present*. Ph.D dissertation, University of Chicago, 1959.

Marriott, Alice L. *Kiowa Years: A Study in Culture Impact*. New York: Macmillan, 1986.

———. *The Ten Grandmothers*. Norman: University of Oklahoma Press, 1945.

Momaday, N. Scott. *The Way to Rainy Mountain*. Albuquerque: University of New Mexico Press, 1969.

Mooney, James. *Calendar History of the Kiowa Indians*. Washington, D.C.: Bureau of American Ethnology Annual Report 17 (1895–96), pt. 1, 1898.

Richardson, Jane. *Law and Status Among the Kiowa Indians*. New York: American Ethnological Society, 1940.

THE KIOWA AT A GLANCE

TRIBE *Kiowa*

CULTURE AREA *Great Plains*

GEOGRAPHY *South Plains of Oklahoma and Texas*

LINGUISTIC FAMILY *Kiowan*

CURRENT POPULATION *approximately 8,500*

FIRST CONTACT *René-Robert Cavelier, Sieur de La Salle, French, 1682*

FEDERAL STATUS *recognized, no reservation. The largest concentration of Kiowa live in the town of Carnegie, in Caddo County, Oklahoma. Many Kiowa also live in Tillman, Cotton, Comanche, Stephens, and Jefferson counties, all in southwestern Oklahoma.*

GLOSSARY

agent A person appointed by the Bureau of Indian Affairs to supervise U.S. government programs on a reservation and/or in a specific region; after 1908 the title "superintendent" replaced "agent."

allotment The U.S. policy, first applied in 1887, of breaking up tribally-owned reservations by assigning individual farms and ranches to Indians. Intended as much to discourage traditional communal activities as to encourage private farming and assimilate Indians into mainstream American life.

American Indian Exposition A powwow (festival) held each year in Anadarko, Oklahoma, to showcase Indian crafts, dancing, and sports.

anthropology The study of the physical, social, and cultural characteristics of human beings.

assimilation Adoption by individuals of the customs of another society; a means by which the host society recruits new members. The United States, as well as most American Indian societies, gained new members in this manner.

band A loosely organized group of people who live in one area and are bound together by the need for food and defense, by family ties, or by other common interests.

bison Large, nondomesticated mammals related to cattle, which lived in vast herds on the Great Plains of the United States until their numbers were sharply diminished by overhunting in the late 19th century. Bison, commonly called buffalo, provided the main ingredients for the major aspects of Plains Indian culture, including food, shelter, clothing, and ritual items.

Bureau of Indian Affairs (BIA) A U.S. government agency within the Department of the Interior. Originally intended to manage trade and other relations with Indians, the BIA now seeks, through the programs it develops and implements, to encourage Indians to manage their own affairs and to improve their educational opportunities and general social and economic well-being.

Carlisle Indian School A federally funded boarding school in Pennsylvania. Young Indians of many tribes who were sent there during the late 19th and early 20th centuries were forced to assimilate into white culture.

civilization program U.S. policy of the late 19th and early 20th centuries designed to change the Indians' way of life so that it resembled that of non-Indians. These programs usually focused on converting Indians to Christianity and encouraging them to become farmers.

clan A multigenerational group having a shared identity, organization, and property, based on belief in descent from a common, often mythical, ancestor. Because clan members consider themselves closely related, marriage within the clan is strictly prohibited.

Ghost Dance movement A religious and cultural revival movement that spread among Indians in the 1870s and centered on the belief that non-Indian newcomers would disappear and the Indians' traditional world would return if certain rituals were performed. Among the Kiowa and some other tribes, these rituals included dances that were performed for days at a time.

Great Plains A flat, dry region in central North America, primarily covered by lush grasslands, which has been the home of the Kiowa throughout their history.

horticulture Food production using human muscle power and simple hand tools to plant and harvest domesticated crops.

Ice Age A time in the earth's past when vast ice sheets or glaciers expanded to cover much of North America and Eurasia and periodically retreated and advanced again. The most recent Ice Age began about 18,000 years ago and ended about 10,000 years ago.

Indian Claims Commission (ICC) A U.S. government body created by an act of Congress in 1946 to hear and rule on claims brought by Indians against the United States. These claims stem from unfulfilled treaty terms, such as nonpayment for lands sold by the Indians.

Indian New Deal Program inaugurated by the Indian Reorganization (Wheeler-Howard) Act of 1934, designed to remove government restrictions on Indian traditions and to encourage autonomous development of Indian communities.

Kwu'-da The Kiowa's name for themselves, meaning "pulling out" or "coming out."

medicine bundle A collection of sacred objects, usually contained in a hide bag, which the Kiowa believed to be the source of tribal and/or individual power, or "medicine."

Native American Church The North American Indian religious organization to which Kiowa Peyote congregations belong. Church practices incorporate aspects of both Christianity and Native American religion. The ceremonies and rituals of the Native American Church center on the use of the hallucinogenic peyote cactus.

Northern Kiowa A small group of Kiowa who tried to stay in the Black Hills, in what is now North Dakota, after most of the Kiowa left for the southern Plains in the 1780s. The Northern Kiowa rejoined their kin in the early 1800s.

Paleo-Indian period The period in North America lasting until about 10,000 years ago. At that time human ways of life involved hunting and gathering food and making specialized stone tools.

palynology The study of plant pollen to determine changes in the environment through time.

peyote A button or fruit of the saguaro cactus plant that is native to Texas, New Mexico, Arizona, and the northern Mexican states and is used as the vehicle or channel of prayer in the Native American Church.

prehistory Anything that happened before written records existed for a given locality. In North America, anything earlier than the first contact with Europeans is considered to be prehistoric.

prestige societies Military, religious, and medicinal groups to which Kiowa belonged. Membership in these societies was based on the skills, talents, and spirit-power possessed by an individual.

relocation The policy of the federal government to encourage Indians to leave the tribal environment of the reservation and migrate to the cities in order to enter mainstream society. This policy was carried out in the 1950s and 1960s under the Voluntary Relocation Program and the Employment Assistance Program.

Sand Creek Massacre The 1864 killing by the territorial militia of peaceful Cheyenne and Arapaho Indians camped along Sand Creek in what is now southeastern Colorado.

Saynday The supernatural being believed by the Kiowa to have brought them into the world and taught them how to survive.

Sun Dance The annual religious and cultural renewal ceremony of the Kiowa and other Indian nations. Because the ritual involved the use of a buffalo, it could no longer be held after the buffalo population declined in the late 1800s.

tai-me The most sacred object of the Kiowa, consisting of green stone decorated with white feathers, used in the Sun Dance and other rituals.

termination Federal policy to remove Indian tribes from government supervision and Indian lands from trust status, in effect from the late 1940s through the 1960s.

tipi A conical, portable shelter made of poles and covered with buffalo hides; the principal dwelling of most Plains Indians, including the Kiowa.

travois A transportation device, made of two poles crossed and tied at one end to form a V, to which supplies and belongings were secured. The travois was at first pulled by dogs and later, after the Kiowa learned to handle them, by horses.

treaty A contract negotiated between representatives of the United States or another national government and one or more Indian tribes. Treaties dealt with surrender of political independence, peaceful relations, boundaries, terms of land sales, and related matters.

tribe A society consisting of several or many separate communities united by kinship, culture, and language, and such other social units as clans, religious organizations, and economic and political institutions.

trust The relationship between the federal government and many Indian tribes, dating from the late 19th century. Government agents managed Indians' business dealings, including land transactions and rights to natural resources, because the Indians were alleged to be legally incompetent to manage their own affairs.

Wounded Knee Massacre The U.S. Army's killing of Sioux Indians in 1890 after their participation in a Ghost Dance held outside their reservation boundaries.

ACKNOWLEDGMENTS

Poem (page 95) courtesy of N. Scott Momaday. Reprinted from *The Way to Rainy Mountain,* © 1969, The University of New Mexico Press.
"Tanning a Hide," courtesy of Maurice Boyd. Reprinted from *Kiowa Voices,* Vol. I., © 1981, Texas Christian University Press.

PICTURE CREDITS

AP/Worldwide Photos, page 95; Courtesy of Maurice Boyd, *Kiowa Voices: Ceremonial Dance, Music, and Song,* Vol. I, and *Kiowa Voices: Myths, Legends, and Folktales,* Vol. II, Texas Christian University Press, 1981 and 1983, pages 41, 48, 51, 59, 70, 79; Courtesy of Carson County Square House Museum, R. C. Cline Collection, pages 82, 86–87; Courtesy of R. C. Cline Land Co., Inc., R. C. Cline, president; Courtesy of Colorado Historical Society, page 50; Cumberland Historical Society, page 74; Department of Anthropology, Smithsonian Institution, cover; Fort Sill Museum, Oklahoma, page 16; Photo by George Kew, University of Virginia, page 101; Library of Congress, pages 42, 60; Lowie Museum of Anthropology, University of California, Berkeley, page 27; Courtesy of James and Helen McCorprin, page 67; Courtesy of N. Scott Momaday, page 44; Museum of the American Indian/Heye Foundation, page 81; National Archives, pages 63, 66; National Museum of American Art, pages 22, 33, 49; Oklahoma Historical Society (Archives and Manuscripts Division), pages 24, 78 (Museum of the Western Prairie), page 97; Susie Peters Collection, Courtesy of Helen McCorprin, Houston, pages 30, 94; Smithsonian Institution, National Anthropological Archives, pages 12, 18, 19, 28, 31, 34, 52, 53, 58, 68, 71, 73, 75, 82–85, 89, 91, 92; South Dakota State Historical Society, page 40; Courtesy of the Anthropology Department, Texas A&M University, page 15; Texas Tech University (Southwest Collection), page 54 (International Center), page 102; U.S. Department of the Interior, Indian Arts and Crafts Board, Southern Plains Museum and Crafts Center, pages 20, 29, 37, 38, 46, 62, 65, 72, 76.

Maps (pages 21, 57, 69) by Gary Tong.

JOHN R. WUNDER is professor of history and director of the Center for Great Plains Studies at the University of Nebraska, Lincoln. He holds a J.D. degree from the University of Iowa and Ph.D. in history from the University of Washington. He is the author of *Inferior Courts, Superior Justice: A History of the Justices of the Peace on the Northwest Frontier*, *At Home on the Range*, *Working the Ranger*, and other books and articles. His main research concerns are Native American history, the history of the Great Plains, and American legal history.

FRANK W. PORTER III, general editor of INDIANS OF NORTH AMERICA, is director of the Chelsea House Foundation for American Indian Studies. He holds a B.A., M.A., and Ph.D. from the University of Maryland. He has done extensive research concerning the Indians of Maryland and Delaware and is the author of numerous articles on their history, archaeology, geography, and ethnography. He was formerly director of the Maryland Commission on Indian Affairs and American Indian Research and Resource Institute, Gettysburg, Pennsylvania, and he has received grants from the Delaware Humanities Forum, the Maryland Committee for the Humanities, the Ford Foundation, and the National Endowment for the Humanities, among others. Dr. Porter is the author of *The Bureau of Indian Affairs* in the Chelsea House KNOW YOUR GOVERNMENT series.